STUDIES IN PUBLIC ADMINISTRATION No. 13

Administration in New Zealand's
Multi - racial Society

*Out of print.

Administration in New Zealand's Multi-racial Society

edited by

R. H. BROOKES and I. H. KAWHARU

★

1967

WELLINGTON - NEW ZEALAND INSTITUTE OF
PUBLIC ADMINISTRATION

★

LONDON - OXFORD UNIVERSITY PRESS

Printed by Wright & Carman Limited, Wellington

Contents

Introduction

I. H. KAWHARU

In 1966 the New Zealand Institute of Public Administration's annual convention, held at Auckland, was addressed by a panel of experts who had been invited to examine the administrative implications of New Zealand's multi-racial society. This volume contains, in an edited form, the papers which were presented on that occasion. Four of them are by administrators, and deal in the main with the ways in which certain government programmes and areas of policy-making are conditioned by the existence in New Zealand of ethnic groups with specific needs. The other two are by academics, whose concern is less with how immediate and specific problems are being solved than with the influence which such solutions may have on the long-term development of New Zealand society, and of the groups of which it is composed.

Arrangements had been made to include in the panel of speakers a senior administrator who was himself a Maori. Unfortunately circumstances obliged him to withdraw. While it is obvious that the remaining participants are well-informed about, and well-disposed towards, the Maori and the other ethnic minorities in New Zealand, it seems appropriate that in writing this introduction I should take the opportunity of presenting a Maori point of view, and in doing so I shall, as an academic, be concerned mainly with the long-range policy alternatives which are discussed in the papers by Dr Metge and Professor Ritchie.

Mr Mardle has made clear in his paper the diversity of national and ethnic minorities which, together with the majority whose ancestors came from the British Isles, form the New Zealand nation. By commonly classifying New Zealanders as 'European' and 'Maori', the notion is fostered that all non-European groups are somehow alike. About all they do share, however, is the lack of a European cultural heritage and racial origin. Between the Maori and the Islander or the Asian (including immigrants from Fiji of Indian stock), ties of local identification are greatly different, though the differences may diminish in significance the more the Maori shares with the others the experience of migration to the city. From social, demographic and administrative points of view, Asian groups in New Zealand seem as yet to be of limited interest, in that they seek no special recognition on racial or cultural grounds. The Islander's position in these respects is intermediate between those of the Maori and the Asian, though inclined if anything, to resemble more closely that of the first-generation Maori immigrant to the city in the calls he makes upon administrative services. In directing my attention to the future of the Maori in New Zealand I shall thus be concentrating on only part of the problem of our multi-racial society, though in political and human terms as well as numerically it is the most important part.

Dr Metge in her paper has distinguished several broad policy alternatives, on which Professor Ritchie has also commented. An important merit of such an approach is that it helps to make explicit the value-assumptions which are embedded in programmes and policies, and so to lay them open to more effective scrutiny and review. It would be futile to deny ourselves the use of such value-loaded concepts as 'integration'; without them we should have no value-premises for analysis itself, or for the practical conclusions which derive from analysis. But it is important to recognise that such concepts do not necessarily provide a sufficient basis for an informed choice between policy alternatives. They may for instance contain latent ambiguities, hence stand in need of still further analysis. As Professor Ritchie points out, the term 'integration', has 'great flexibility, but poor directive definition', and while this may be an advantage (as he suggests) in some respects, it is liable to create misunderstandings if different racial groups interpret it in different ways. Dr Metge's comment, that many Maoris suspect that integration is only another name for assimilation, is significant in this regard. Multi-racial support for programmes and policies cannot safely be grounded on ambiguities in the concepts used to justify them.

A pakeha formulated his ideal for New Zealand's bi-racial society in 1840, with the benediction *he iwi kotahi tatou* ('We are one people'). A century and a quarter later, members of his race are still attempting to define the values of our multi-racial society; but as views differed as to the meaning of the ideal in the forties of the nineteenth century, so they continue to differ in the sixties of the twentieth century, not only between Maori and pakeha, but among the pakehas themselves.

Today, as Mr McEwen's paper makes clear, the policy of the Government is one of integration:

> . . . the present Government policy interprets integration as a state of affairs where no citizen differs from any other citizen, because of his ethnic origin, in his economic and social rights, opportunities and responsibilities. On the other hand the policy of integration does not mean that an individual is not free to choose his own cultural pursuits; it does not mean that Maoris will be compelled to abandon their own historical or traditional background.

But Mr McEwen still has to preface his definition with the remark, 'Unfortunately the word "integration" varies in meaning according to the views of the person using it . . .'. Moreover, it is not so very long since the goal was described by an altogether different concept, namely 'assimilation'. Thus Mr Schwimmer, formerly editor of *Te Ao Hou* and Advisory Officer to the Department of Maori Affairs, asserted in 1960 that there had been a policy of *assimilation* ever since 1840. Later in 1960 Mr Hunn, then Secretary for Maori Affairs, after defining 'assimilation' as 'to become absorbed, blended, amalgamated, with complete loss of Maori culture', went on to note that:

> In the course of centuries, Britain passed through integration to assimilation. Signs are not wanting that that may be the destiny of the two races in New Zealand in the distant future.

It is accordingly hardly surprising if, in Mr McEwen's words, 'many Europeans obviously treat "integration" and "assimilation" as synonyms'. The elaboration of definitions to distinguish between alternative concepts of policy may clarify our understanding, but it helps to show that we understand different things about the kind of multi-racial society towards which we should be working. Too many of us have been assuming too much for too long.

This is true not only of the definition of objectives, but also of assumptions about the nature of ethnic groups and of the social changes which they are experiencing. An adequate understanding in these fields too is necessary before one can make an informed choice between policy alternatives. I have in mind here not the general assumption that it is the Maori who is to become part of pakeha society, instead of the other way round: given the political situation and the difference in size of the two populations it is inevitable that changes in beliefs and behaviour will be more rapid and more radical among the Maori than the pakeha. Too little thought however has been given to the nature and implications of such changes in evaluating the broad policy alternatives.

The point can be illustrated by comparing two forms of integration. On the one hand one could envisage a process of integration between two Maori tribes (the Arawa, say, with the Tuwharetoa) for certain political and economic purposes. Such a process might not be easy to achieve, yet it is simple to conceive, since the kinship basis of Maori society (the tribe) would not be affected. Indeed, an example of such integration for certain specific (military) purposes can be seen in the Maori Battalion; the tribe was the very basis for its recruitment and mobilisation in two World Wars. In other words, in the context of Maori social organisation 'integration' means the combining of two or more kin-groups into a whole for certain limited purposes, each of the component parts retaining its identity.

But to integrate, say the Arawa with the pakeha poses conceptual problems—let alone practical ones—of a quite different order. What in pakeha society is the counterpart of the tribe? Integration in this context can only mean the combining of *individuals* into a bi-racial group (e.g. a suburban community). Accordingly, current administrative programmes (such as individualised aid in housing, land settlement, trade training, vocational guidance) can make sense only on pakeha terms; one of the component parts does not retain its identity since the process of individualisation erodes the tribal basis of the Maori group.

It is therefore not surprising that at the Auckland convention at which these papers were presented, the sense of assurance (mentioned by Professor Ritchie) which was apparent in the discussion of programmes of economic integration was markedly absent when the other supposed plank of integration policy—the preservation of Maori culture—was discussed. The cultural field, with all that it entails in the matter of identity, has been barren of development, since Maori cultural institutions are tribally based, and current programmes of integration do not preserve the tribal structure.

How far has this process of erosion gone? First we must distinguish between Maoris in urban and in rural areas. While both groups are undergoing change, the latter still retains some semblance of tribal identity, while the former does not. Changes in traditional institutions in tribal communities may be termed organisational. They are changes of detail and of process, due largely to increasing involvement in a money economy and to the absorption of Western technology, and they have not yet resulted in radical changes in basic ideology or in the structure of social roles. But the individual who moves out of the tribal context and into the town, finds himself part of a totally different social system. His ties with non-kin are now far more numerous, and many of his social interests are satisfied by entirely different relationships, if not by entirely different institutions. And the values of one do not necessarily hold in the other.

This dichotomy between rural and urban, tribal and non-tribal, is not absolute; yet the distinction is real enough. Furthermore, it is one which is commonly overlooked by those who believe that all modern Maori are detribalised (whatever that may mean), and by those who minister to individuals as if the only socio-cultural milieu now worth considering is that of the pakeha. Granted then that it would be possible to maintain Maori culture in rural areas, is it possible to recreate it in the towns?

Generally, the Maori who migrates to the town or city finds himself a member of a relatively large-scale society, caught up for varying periods of time in a series of non-overlapping networks of impersonal relationships. As in the case of shopkeepers and customers, social roles tend to be functionally specific and affectively neutral; they apply to everyone, regardless of origin, and may be of short duration. What is often important—as for instance between factory-hand and management—is efficiency of performance and the rights and obligations of contract, not criteria of status ascribed by genealogy and validated by a non-European cultural tradition. As there are more ways of life in a large-scale than in a small-scale society, so there may be less consistency between the separate systems of social values. Thus the migrant will not only find more ways of doing things, and a wider range of rewards and penalties, but also something he has never known before: anonymity and loneliness. It is not surprising that the new environment poses a challenge to his sense of identity and self-respect.

However, it follows that so long as he feels himself to be in alien surroundings and faced with half-understood choices, social groupings with a relatively high degree both of consistency in their values, and of cohesiveness in their organisation, should attract and hold him. Kinship and friendship are groupings of just this kind, and it is they (rather than the formal organisations of government and commerce, of religion and recreation) which may provide a basis for an urban Maori culture.

It should be noted first that ties of kinship and friendship between the migrant and his community of origin may be of more than passing consequence. One reason for the persistence of these ties, even well beyond the first generation migrant, is the system of inheritance. For the urban Maori, at least, succession to a land interest may serve as an insurance against a complete severance of ties to a tribal community. Moreover, rural Maori or Island communities may well take care to maintain the links with urban kin and friends, in anticipation of their own possible future migration, or that of their children; again, insurance in a uncertain world.

Within the urban area, kinship may continue to have meaning for the migrant in at least two contexts. First he may maintain relations with other kin in a domestic household; for though kinship in the urban or suburban household is kinship of a most truncated kind, it may still have vital meaning for the migrant. The family remains the most economic mechanism for meeting such needs as the provision of shelter, food, child care and so forth. Furthermore, it gives emotional satisfaction through a broader sense of identity, in a way that few jobs can give; indeed, the less meaningful the content of the migrant's work, the more the family may help to restore his sense of purpose.

Second, kinship can have meaning for the migrant in the work situation. It is true that here kinsmen may become parasitic upon one another (though by the same token, kin sanctions may be brought to bear against offenders quite independently of 'organisation' sanctions). Equally, however, kinsmen may well support one another against adversity, or the threat of it.

Unlike kinship, which is ascribed, friendship is a relationship which is achieved. To understand why friendships tend to form among members of the same racial group, the motives for achieving them must be understood, and for this purpose we can make use of a distinction (suggested by Wolf) between emotional and instrumental kinds of friendship. As a working hypothesis to explain the former, it may be supposed that the emotional content provides a release from the strains of conforming to a role circumscribed by alien rules, and enforced by alien and sometimes hostile personnel. Research is needed into the conditions under which friendships of this type tend to form; conditions on the waterfront and among construction gangs and transport workers, appear to offer promising fields of enquiry.

Instrumental friendship, on the other hand, is the type of relationship in which the participants stand to maximise their opportunities of gaining access to physical or social resources. It is characterised by reciprocity; if an imbalance develops, the friendship may well rupture. Such relationships are found among Maori and Island urban migrants to the extent that a common racial identity succeeds in supplanting a common tribal identity. Again, research is necessary into the patterns of status, authority, influence and control among such groups.

These proposals for research are merely specific illustrations of the general point made by Professor Ritchie:

> . . . we vitally need more sociological research to tell us what the urban community is like, in human and social terms, so that we can find ways of replacing the functions which peasant community served by appropriate community functions in the city.

Until that research has been done, and a number of social experiments made, it would be unwise dogmatically to assert, either that urbanisation must inevitably destroy Maori culture and values, or that through kinship and friendship groups they can survive and develop. All I am concerned here to insist is that we should recognise the difference between the possible consequences of an evolutionary trend and the certain implications of an administrative policy, and that we should not surrender our freedom of choice over the latter by too readily making assumptions about the former. Of course it is natural in a pakeha society that government programmes should have taken the form of individualised aid rather than of maintaining and working through the tribal organisation; but it does not follow that that is the only practicable form they could take. It would be possible to build up, side by side with the existing administrative structure, one which worked through the tribes or (in the cities) through evolving communities based on kinship and friendship. However, the total absence of any such alternative is the clearest indication to the Maori that when the pakeha says integration, he really means assimilation.

The absence of official alternatives does not of course imply that a Maori individual or group has no choice. He can choose to operate outside the limits of a State aid programme, and a few do so. But even fewer succeed, since courses of action (say, in rural housing, or agriculture) which are outside the scope of State policy frequently encounter insuperable financial or technical obstacles. If the Maori are to preserve their institutions on a sound economic base, they must (initially, at least) do so with the support of the State, not outside or against it.

It is for this reason that a Maori contribution, equivalent to that of the pakeha, to the definition of the form which our multi-racial society can and should take is so necessary. What statements on integration have been made by Maoris on behalf of the Maori people to match those of successive Ministers and Secretaries of Maori Affairs? Do individual Maoris and pakehas speak of the same goal when they speak of integration, and if not, which goal has become policy, and why?

To sum up: choices between the long-range policy alternatives distinguished by Dr Metge and Professor Ritchie should be preceded by a genuine dialogue in which both Maori and pakeha must take a full part; but this discussion about what should be done can be meaningful only to the extent that research has shown what can in fact be done. In the meantime, options should be assumed to be open until they have been shown to be closed. And it is vital that the researchers and decision-makers should be sufficiently aware of the interrelationships in the life of social groups—that one cannot deal with any aspect in isolation, hence, for instance that one cannot in one's socio-economic programmes erode the kinship basis of Maori society and still expect to preserve and develop the Maori culture which is based on it.

From the papers which follow we can form an estimate of what progress we have made with these tasks, and how far we have yet to go. For this reason, and irrespective of their other merits, they will be welcomed by all who are concerned for the quality of the administration of New Zealand's growing multi-racial society.

The Growth of a Multi-racial Society in New Zealand

R. J. MARDLE

The population of New Zealand at the time of the last published census (1961) comprised almost 92 percent Europeans, a little under 7 percent of Maoris,[1] and 1.3 percent of people from a large number of other racial or national origins. The Europeans were predominantly from the British Isles or born in New Zealand of British stock—what proportion precisely it is impossible to say, but a rough estimate on the information available is that about 88 percent of the population came within this category, leaving about 4 percent of or descended from other European nationalities. Because people of British origin or descent predominate in our society, I shall regard all others as the minority groups in our multi-racial society.

The figure of about 7 percent for the Maori population is probably understated in consequence of the definitions and procedures associated with the census, while the proportion with at least one Maori ancestor is considerably larger still. Many of

---

[1] Where numbers of Maoris are quoted in this paper, unless otherwise indicated, the census definition of a Maori is used i.e. a person describing himself as having half to full Maori blood. The number of completely full-blooded Maoris in the census totals is known to be overstated. There is some census information on the number of persons of less than half Maori blood, who are arbitrarily counted in the non-Maori population.

part-Maori ancestry would be almost fully assimilated into the European population and would class themselves in that category. However, it seems reasonable to say that at the time of the 1961 census, for practical purposes between 12 and 15 percent of the population were in the minority groups as defined above, rather more than half being New Zealand Maoris and the rest of various European, Asian, Polynesian, and other origins.

The proportion of our society consisting of Maoris and of people of other non-European races has increased noticeably in the last 25 years or so, having almost doubled between 1936 and 1961. Persons of European nationalities other than British have also increased markedly since the Second World War. This process has continued since the 1961 census and the latest figures for the 1966 census record a Maori population of over 201,000, representing an increase of over 34,000 or 20 percent in five years. Accurate calculations of the immigration since 1961 of non-Europeans, and of Europeans other than British, together with estimates of their natural increase in New Zealand, are not easy to make, and the 1966 census figures have not yet been published in full. However, it would seem that since 1961 the expansion in numbers of the minority groups, including Maoris, accounts for something like 25 percent of the aggregate population growth. The Maori population increase accounted for about 13 percent and a similar proportion probably came from the non-Maori minority groups. This means, of course, that our society is becoming still more multi-racial in character.

Having outlined the present situation we can pose some questions. How did this multi-racial society come about? Where did the minority groups come from? Where are they located in the country? In what occupational groups are they found? To what extent are they assimilated into the general community, or do they remain as isolated pockets? What policies are currently being followed in their admission to New Zealand? These are some of the questions that this background paper will endeavour to answer, to the extent that limitations of space permit.

This figure is substantially understated, as there are many persons who either do not know they have some Maori ancestry or how much, and describe themselves as Europeans, Chinese, etc. Moreover, many who have less than half Maori blood nevertheless live as part of the Maori community and have similar outlooks and characteristics. Consequently, the Maori content of the population is much larger than the official figures suggest. (See Population Census 1961, Vol. 8, Maori Population and Dwellings, Introduction pp. 3-14.)

Fall and rise of the Maori people

Since they form the largest minority group we shall consider the Maori people first. It may seem a strange question to ask nowadays, when they constitute quite a small fraction of the total community, but we must ask it: how did the Maori people become a minority at all? It is quite clear that in the early days of European settlement they were a very substantial majority: a strong, virile, proud, healthy, and fairly adaptable people who, had they continued to increase at a normal rate, would by this time have had a population of considerable size.

But, as Sinclair[2] says, 'when they began to feel the weight of Western civilization pressing on their lives, they began to pass through a moral and technological revolution more comprehensive and more painful than contemporary industrialisation in Europe'. Divided by tribal jealousies and animosities, with no unifying leadership, their traditional economic and cultural mores so very different from those of the more highly-developed and comparatively well-organised society which bore upon them, innocent of Western economic values, their simple standards of honour much above the low dealings of European exploiters, they were no match for the newcomers.

They became grossly affected and disillusioned by the injustice, harshness or mere stupidity of the treatment they received, first at the hands of unscrupulous traders and early residents, who scarcely represented the best of European culture and all too often showed its worst, then through the avaricious dealings of the land sharks, and a little later through the continued questionable acquisition of their lands by the settlement companies partly in consequence of the muddlement of official policies. Their primitive weapons were replaced by the far more lethal firearms and thus their inter-tribal conflicts, once relatively harmless (a little like Rugby football, governed by accepted rules but with occasional resort to rougher measures), now became savage massacres. Maori numbers were decimated by this wanton destruction and by wars with the pakeha, also by the tragic ravages of imported epidemic and infectious diseases against which their primitive ideas of hygiene and medical care were woefully inadequate.

For over 50 years they were psychologically dispirited by defeat, by their declining numbers, by tribal disorganisation, by alienation

---

[2] Sinclair, K. *A History of New Zealand*, Penguin Books, 1959, p. 40.

from their lands through sale and confiscation, by the impact of Western ideas and religion upon their culture, by forms of law and order which they could not understand and which cut across older patterns of Maori thought and behaviour, by political and administrative government in which they had practically no say, by a sense of inferiority arising from their lack of a written language and literature and a vast accumulation of knowledge comparable to that of Western civilisation, and by numerical and economic submergence. It seemed that the gloomy findings of the 1837 report of the Committee of the British House of Commons on the conditions and welfare of 'aborigines' were being confirmed yet again—that colonisation resulted for non-European peoples in calamity and even extermination.[3]

The consequences for the Maori people today are not always fully realised. First, although we are now 150 years distant from these early beginnings of one race's impact upon another, the emotional, psychological, cultural and economic conflicts—while substantially ameliorated—have still been far from resolved. Second, the effect on the size of the Maori population was nothing short of catastrophic. From quite early in European settlement the numbers of Maoris rapidly declined. For information on these numbers we are dependent upon various estimates which do not agree, some being not much more than guesses from very partial contacts. The highest was 200,000 by the missionary Williams in 1835; the most detailed was that of Dr Dieffenbach whose estimate of 114,890 in 1842 ought probably to be taken as a minimum, for a population already affected by armed warfare. A not unreasonable conservative figure for about 1840 may be the 120,000 given in the New Zealand Colonial Blue Books.

At the beginning of the 1840s the Maori population outnumbered European settlers by over 20 to 1. While the earliest censuses of the Maori population cannot be regarded as very reliable it is clear that within 20 years the number of Maoris had been reduced by about a half, and further slow contraction brought them to not much over 40,000 by the end of the century. The relative position had been completely reversed, non-Maoris now outnumbering Maoris by 17 to 1. Instead of 2,000 Maoris to every 100 non-Maoris, the proportion had fallen to only 6 to 100. Notwithstanding a slow but steady recovery over the next 25 years the proportion of Maoris declined further still.

---

[3] Sinclair, op. cit. p. 61.

The reanimation of spirit that began about 1900 occurred as benevolent governments endeavoured to help them, as the Maoris themselves rediscovered their past through the work of European scholars, and as their vitality and sense of identity were 'stimulated further by the emergence of some notable and learned young leaders'.[4] Such change within could only be gradual in effect, but from 1926 the upward trend accelerated. In the next 40 years the numbers more than trebled. Nevertheless, it was not until comparatively recent times that the former peak numbers of well over a century ago have been regained. Even though the Maoris have experienced a rate of natural increase higher than that of non-Maoris for at least the last 40 years (and more than double in most years) the ratio of Maoris to others is still only 7.5 to 100.

How different it could have been! What the rate of Maori population growth might have been if European settlement had not had such unfortunate results is conjectural. Since 1931, the rate of natural increase among Maoris has been below 2 percent in only one year, and has on occasion exceeded 4 percent. Let us imagine, however, that Maori population would have grown at the comparatively low average rate of 2 percent per year: it would have doubled every 35 years, and by the turn of the century would have been 10 times what it actually was. By now it would be approaching no less than 1,500,000. Had the average rate of increase been as high as 2½ percent, Maoris would equal the present total population of about 2,700,000. These 'ifs' are subject to many qualifications, yet at least they suggest the order of magnitude, and significance for the Maori people, of the calamity that occurred.

Some characteristics of the Maori population

Having examined in brief the history of the Maori minority in our population, it is desirable to set down some of its present characteristics in summary form. Most of these have implications, evident or potential, for race relations.

(1) As recently as 1936, 90 percent of Maoris lived in rural areas. Since then, and especially since the Second World War, there has been a growing tendency for them to move to the cities and towns and to increase there. Nevertheless, in 1961 two-thirds were still rurally domiciled, away from the main areas of population and employment, and a majority still are.

---

[4] Watson, J. E. *Horizons of Unknown Power: Some Issues of Maori Schooling*, N.Z. Council for Educational Research, Wellington 1965, p. 14.

(2) In some areas Maoris constitute a much larger part of the population than they do elsewhere. Three-quarters of all Maoris live in the northern half of the North Island. In the East Coast area they make up nearly a third of the population, in Northland nearly a quarter, and in South Auckland/Bay of Plenty a sixth. Within these areas, and in some others, are many localities where they comprise 50 percent of the population. In a few localities, notably on the East Coast, Maoris are actually in the majority. The locations of high Maori population density are away from the main industrial areas, although in the Northland and South Auckland/Bay of Plenty areas there has been significant recent industrial development.

(3) The older generation of Maoris tends to be conservative and traditional in outlook, trying to preserve old patterns of life and culture. A large proportion of them live in country areas. The younger generation, better educated and bursting in numbers, having wider contacts with pakeha society, tends to be impatient of some of the entangling cobwebs of the past, yet often maintains at least partially the ties of tribe, family and kin, and bows to older authority in a way typical of Maori communities.[5] More than half the Maoris aged 20–34 now live in the towns.

(4) The recency of urban migration has created problems of social and vocational adjustment in the cities, including some social disorganisation, racial discrimination and inequality.[6] These consequences are scarcely surprising, in view of the more than tenfold increase in the number of urban Maoris since 1936. This figure may, however, put the picture out of focus. Here are some provisional statistics relating to specific urban areas as at March 1966 to supply a better perspective:

Urban Area	Number of Maoris	Maoris as a Percentage of Urban Population of Area
Auckland	33,261	6.1
Whangarei	3,217	11.0
Hamilton	4,322	6.8
Rotorua	7,109	21.7
Gisborne	4,583	16.5
Wellington	6,159	3.7
All North Island Urban Areas	76,271	6.3

5 See Metge, A. J. *A New Maori Migration: Rural and Urban Relations in Northern New Zealand,* Athlone Press, London, 1964, pp. 106, 127-131.
6 Watson, op. cit., p. 5.

Migration is not only taking place to urban areas, but also from isolated country districts to districts less isolated and to areas near to cities. In some parts of the country the accumulated effect on the remaining population is quite dramatic. In Northland for instance there was an actual decline in Maori population from 1956–61.

(5) Among the reasons given by Watson for the new migration are:

* The weakening of bitterness and suspicion. This cannot be overcome quickly in the older generation who may even put impediments in the way of the younger generation who wish to set out on Dr Metge's 'new migration'.

* Government policies. The Hunn Report and subsequent Government statements make it clear that the future of the Maoris lies where the Europeans are.

* Experience in the armed forces.[7]

* The lure of cities for the younger people, particularly in the light of their restricted opportunities for work and pleasure in the hinterlands.

* The effect of the high Maori birthrate, forcing the population from areas that cannot support a larger population.

* Shrinking land resources. We should link this with the complications of Maori land titles.

(6) With the movement of Maoris into towns, the employment pattern is changing rapidly. For the first time, the 1961 census showed more Maori males (10,532 or over one-quarter) engaged in manufacturing industries than in primary industries. Compared with their total numbers they made a particularly useful contribution to the labour force in food manufacture (especially in meat freezing), in construction and in road transport, as earth-moving equipment operators, and as waterfront workers. Nearly half the Maori women were employed in service industries, but a substantially increased proportion—a third of the total—was employed in manufacturing, and particularly in the production of footwear and clothing. Comparisons with earlier censuses show quite a marked upgrading of Maori skills, although a large proportion are still engaged in unskilled or semi-skilled work. In some areas there is a measure of under-employment, subsistence farming or partial or seasonal employment only. Nevertheless, the Maori is

---

[7] See also Metge, op. cit., p. 105.

beginning to find a widening range of employment opportunities, as employers, faced with acute labour shortages, recognise the reserves of talent and skill awaiting development and use in the Maori population; and as the Maori himself commences to shake off his preoccupation with the present and become concerned about his rightful place in an urban and European society.

(7) The Maori population is characterised by a high birth-rate —one of the highest in the world—and a low death rate. The latter is a little misleading because it is weighted by the youthfulness of the population (50 percent under 15 years of age). Notwithstanding considerable improvement in Maori health in recent years the actual expectation of life for Maoris is 11 years less than for non-Maoris in the case of males and 15 years less in the case of females. The proportional annual death rate for Maoris over 55 years of age is 13 percent higher than for others: the infant mortality rate under one year of age is two and a half times as great as among non-Maoris. Future Maori reproduction is likely to be high as the large number of female children enter the reproductive age groups. It is estimated that the number of Maori women in these age groups will almost double in 15 years.

(8) The average Maori family is much larger and younger than in the rest of the population. As a result over 70 percent of Maoris are dependent upon the 29 percent actively engaged in employment. This size of Maori families tends to overcrowding in homes, where there are 60 percent more occupants per dwelling than among pakehas, yet the latter have a fifth more rooms per home.[8] The financial burden of support leads to a pressure on children to cut their education short, and to begin earning as soon as possible, and this in turn results in a greater degree of blind-alley employment.

(9) Income levels are nearly 30 percent below those of the non-Maori sector. This results from factors already mentioned; from their work distribution being largely in manual occupations or as operatives; from the comparatively low proportions in work requiring higher skills or education, or in managerial or executive posts, or employed on their own account. Because of these lower income levels Maoris have little opportunity to save—a characteristic accentuated by a traditionally 'Mexican' attitude to tomor-

---

8 ibid., pp. 43, 143–153.

row and the day after; they often live in poorer type houses, quite a number of which are officially classed as 'huts, whares and baches'; fewer of them own houses and proportionately more rent them than in the rest of the population; they enjoy fewer amenities in their homes. Compared with pakehas, six times as many Maoris have no hot water service, 10 times as many no bath or shower, four times as many no flush toilet, over twice as many no refrigerator, and two and a half times as many no electric washing machine. Such factors create social distinctions which have nothing to do with ethnic origin or colour of skin, but may easily be confused with these things. Some part of the differences from pakehas in domestic amenities is, of course, due to the large proportion of Maoris who are rural dwellers.

The Maori's economic and social status

Whether Maori or pakeha, children from homes of manual workers tend to respond to concrete, tangible, immediate and particularised values rather than those that are abstract, intangible, or future. In addition, the strong kinship or group relationships characteristic of Maori living, whether in country or town, are carried over into the work world. The Maori is most at home when he can work in a group, and particularly with other Maoris —in labouring gangs for local authorities, in sheep shearing gangs, on large building jobs, in hydro-electric construction work, forestry and logging, meat freezing works, canneries, clothing factories, or in waterfront work. In many instances this group orientation provides also the opportunity he seeks for active open-air types of work rather than sedentary indoor jobs, and for 'practical' work using his hands, strength, or manipulative skills rather than physically inactive mental work requiring analytical thought or clerical or executive responsibility. These influences are often linked with the strong pull younger Maori men feel towards work with mobile machines and heavy vehicles. They revel in driving large trucks, buses, bulldozers, mechanical shovels, digging and excavating machines, carryalls, scrapers, graders, rollers and the like.

It is often assumed that the Maori engages in some kinds of unskilled or semi-skilled work because his level of education fits him for little else. It is overlooked that this is the kind of work he likes, that he is happy in, and that is backed up by a thousand years of development of particular kinds of interpersonal relationships. Moreover, it needs to be said that the readiness of Maoris to do this sort of work has made an important contribution to the economy. Without them such industries as farming, meat freezing, fruit and vegetable processing, building and construction, road maintenance, transport, bush operations, sawmilling, hotel and restaurant work and a number of others would have been woefully short of labour. It is certain that had this contribution not been available, we would have had to 'import' through immigration programmes a very much larger number of persons willing to perform such work, as Australia has had to do.

The small number of Maoris in responsible positions may not be unassociated with the fact that in Maori society the younger generation is accustomed to direction and guidance from the older. Thus the Maori worker is often reluctant to accept responsibility but prefers to be told what to do. A further handicap in securing a responsible job is that the strength of kinship ties is such that the urban Maori in good employment may feel obliged to return to his rural family or relatives, sometimes for quite lengthy periods, to help with seasonal work on the farm. He is almost certain to return for a marriage or death, or even a special *hui*. Often when he has money, he feels no need for more work until it is spent. Absenteeism of this kind is scarcely likely to lead to his economic advancement. If he is a seasonal worker, say in a freezing works, he is much more inclined than his European counterpart to idle away the off-season rather than look for casual work to fill the gap. He tends to be improvident, to buy heavily on hire purchase, and to give little thought to the future or to his self-improvement. Enjoying life is more important to him than getting on in life.

The point is that, while he may be quite happy this way, he does not make his maximum contribution to the economy or to society as a whole, and of course this attitude may also give rise to social problems. The picture others get of him may be that of a person somewhat irresponsible and carefree, and he may come to be regarded by some as a second-rate citizen. These are merely generalisations which concern observed behaviour patterns: the last thing the writer intends them to be is criticism. In understanding the Maori in our society they must nevertheless be mentioned.

The Maori in urbanised society, especially the younger and better educated man, is I believe becoming conscious and not a little sensitive about pakeha judgment concerning how he adjusts to the dominant pakeha society in which he lives. Not only this, but he is being told by his own people that unless he competes successfully in that world he is letting his race down, while at

the same time withdrawal from the pakeha world to become 'more
Maori' is also letting his race down. Watson says: 'the deepest
sources of his conflicts . . . are the community's expectations that
he will value his Maori identity while he is continuously being made
to feel ashamed of it'.[9]

There has been a good deal of discussion of the relative merits
of assimilation, integration, 'parallel development', symbiosis, mis-
cegenation and various other ways in which the differences between
the Maori minority and the rest of the population can be bridged.
It is a large part of the theses of Hunn,[10] Watson and Woods[11]
that mobility and integration will have to be stepped up if the
needs of the immediate future are to be met. Watson has pointed
out[12] that the past history of this issue has been bedevilled by
deliberate segregation, separation or ostracism. This is certainly
no longer generally true, nor has it been for some time. As Watson
says in relation to present policies: 'The Maori people are not
inflamed by white exclusivism. If anything, they are uneasy about
inclusivist policies, for while they have adopted much of the culture of the pakeha they are not yet willing to have their Maori
culture assimilated out of existence.'

Not that this is intended. The promotion and preservation of
Maori culture are an integral plank of official policy.[13] Nevertheless, they are challenged by the actual events of Maori integration,
and especially by the intermarriage of Maoris and non-Maoris.
Maoris of half to less than full blood increased from 29 percent
of the Maori total in 1926 to 38 percent in 1961. Persons known
to be less than half Maori, and therefore counted in the non-Maori
population, have increased even more. If we count all those actually identified in the census as having some Maori ancestry we
find that for every 100 persons who declared themselves to be of
full Maori blood the number with less than full blood has been
in successive censuses as follows:

1926	:	54	1951	:	75
1936	:	68⎱	1956	:	84⎱
1945	:	89⎰	1961	:	95⎰

---

[9] op. cit., p. 32.
[10] Hunn, J. K., *Report on Department of Maori Affairs,* Government
Printer, Wellington, 1961.
[11] Woods, N. S., *Immigration and the Labour Force,* I.D.C. background
paper 26, Government Printer, Wellington, 1960.
[12] op. cit., p. 3.
[13] Hunn, op. cit., p. 15.

The two bracketed periods, those when the greatest change has occurred, are the periods when Europeans and Maoris have been thrown closely together—in the Second World War and in the recent urban migration. This latter movement is not likely to abate. It is not within the scope of this background paper to comment on the general ethnic, sociological and cultural implications of these trends. Obviously, however, the Maori will tend to become more Europeanised and as he does so, more urbanised, more industrialised, probably better educated, and more widely distributed in skilled occupations and professions. More intermarriage will take place. These factors will all interact. Hunn sees urbanisation and its consequences as likely to be the best means of preventing a colour problem from arising in New Zealand as the Maori population expands. Let me conclude this section by quoting from his report:

> People understand and appreciate one another better and mutually adjust themselves easier if living together as neighbours than if living apart in separate communities.

The immigrants

We have chosen to regard the Maoris as an indigenous people although, as is well known, they came in a series of migrations hundreds of years ago from distant Polynesian Islands. The immigrant people who thrust them aside came from Europe, mostly from the British Isles, although the earliest traders were a motley lot of various nationalities.

There have been three distinct periods when the numbers of 'aliens' (for want of a better term) have grown noticeably; at other times they have remained almost static—that is, alien increases and losses have almost balanced, with a slight tilt sometimes one way and sometimes the other. The three chief periods of growth of the non-British, non-Maori population were: (1) the gold-rush heyday of the 1860s, (2) the expansionist Vogel era of public works development and opening up of the hinterland, and (3) the 1950s, when labour shortages were acute.

The census of 1861 enumerated 2,667 aliens in the population, and within three years there were 5,808, rising to 10,000 by 1871. The large inflow of the seventies brought many more. Within 10 years the number of foreign born almost doubled to just under 20,000, but thereafter it slowly declined until in 1936 there were only 15,348. The most rapid change has occurred since the Second

World War, the numbers of aliens reaching 49,000 in the 1961 census, plus an estimated addition of between 30,000 and 40,000 more since then, including now quite a large number of children born here to alien parents.

People from Northern Europe

The 1864 census included 1,999 persons born in Germany, most of whom had come from earlier settlement in Australia. We may also count as Europeans the 1,100 persons born in the United States of America. Both of these groups were gold-rush immigrants. There were 505 settlers from France—an evidence of the early French interest in New Zealand. (There were fewer French in New Zealand 100 years later and only a handful more from Germany.)

In the Vogel era of the seventies and early eighties, 8,000 European immigrants were assisted to New Zealand, of whom the largest groups were German (3,185), Danish (2,009), Norwegian (743), and Swedish (727). Most of the Scandinavians arrived under the 'special settlement' schemes of land development and settled in the Manawatu block and in the Seventy-mile Bush at Norsewood and Dannevirke. These people, except in some cases for their names, are no longer distinguishable from New Zealanders of British stock, with whom they have been fully assimilated.

Independent German immigration continued until 1914: there were 3,400 German settlers between 1900 and 1914, of whom quite a large proportion were originally migrants to Australia who were motivated to leave there by the long economic depression in Australia in the early 1900s. A few German refugees from the Nazi régime arrived before the Second World War, and small numbers have been arriving in recent years.

Dutch immigration was considerable in the 1950s. The first group of 856 came earlier in 1946–47 under the Netherlands East Indies Recuperation Scheme, but the Government's assisted scheme negotiated in 1950 to alleviate labour shortages stimu-lated a sizeable regular intake. The original scheme tailed off as economic conditions in the Netherlands improved until it ceased in 1963, but the Netherlands Government has continued to give financial assistance to all Dutch immigrants and the New Zealand Government has subsidised the transport costs of workers in sel-ected, categories. However, the majority of arrivals from the Netherlands—as from Britain—have not come under the main assisted scheme, there being 6,261 arrivals attributable to the latter out of 25,124 Dutch immigrants from April 1950 to March 1965. These people have proved excellent settlers and have integrated with the rest of the community with ease. They are marrying New Zealanders and are already scarcely separable from the bulk of the population.

Southern European and Mediterranean group

A few hundred Italians arrived under Government schemes from 1875 to 1877, and a small uneven flow has continued but only from a few Italian villages. There is a large Italian 'colony' in Wellington and the rest have predominantly settled in Auckland, Napier and Canterbury. They have retained a fair measure of their national identity, maintained contacts with relatives in Italy, and there is some traffic to and fro. According to Lochore[14] they do not become 'New Zealanders' until the second New Zealand-born generation.

The first Yugoslavs (mainly Dalmatians) came later than the Italians, worked in Northland gumfields and later settled on some of the poorer lands. Today about 80 percent are found about Auckland and in Northland. There have been additions since the war through the arrival of 504 Yugoslavian displaced persons, and recently through a small regular intake. These people integrate slowly but provide few problems.

Very few people came from Hungary before 280 displaced persons were admitted after the Second World War. Subsequently, after the Hungarian uprising of 1956, another 1,117 refugees were admitted. Nearly 90 percent are located in the four main urban areas.

Greeks have been coming to New Zealand in small numbers for many years but there has been somewhat of an upward surge since the Second World War, partly through the assisted migration of about 300 Greek girls. Over 70 percent of Greeks are located in Wellington where they comprise a strong national community, with their own institutions. Like Italians, they tend to retain close ties with their homeland, while their Greek Orthodox faith distinguishes them from most of the rest of the community.

Syrians and Lebanese are an old-established racial group in New Zealand. Most of them live in or around the cities, notably in

---

[14] Lochore, R. A. *From Europe to New Zealand,* Reed, Wellington, 1951.

Auckland, Wellington and Dunedin, and an unusually large proportion is engaged in commercial activity. In the 1961 census, 1,082 came within this racial group but 84 percent were born in New Zealand and over half were of mixed blood, demonstrating that the original migration took place many years ago. The surprising thing is that they retain their separate identity, which suggests that in spite of the considerable amount of intermarriage, they do not assimilate very readily into the majority population.

Eastern Europe

New Zealand has had very little immigration from Eastern Europe. However, during 1949 to 1953 some 4,800 displaced persons from Europe were admitted by arrangement with the International Refugee Organisation. Excluding those mentioned above, the principal countries of origin or last residence were: Rumania 918, Poland 847, Latvia 545, Czechoslovakia 336, U.S.S.R. 275, Lithuania 242, Bulgaria 199, Estonia 189, Ukraine 179. Special reception and rehabilitation camps were set up to give them basic training in English, customs, government, law, etc. Since then a trickle has come from Eastern Europe, mainly to reunite families or on other humanitarian grounds.

Chinese

The gold-rush brought the first considerable number of Chinese to New Zealand, initially from Australia but later direct from China. The census of 1874 recorded 4,814 Chinese residents, of whom only two were women. The view then current of the 'yellow peril' combined with understandable concern at the sex imbalance of the Chinese minority in New Zealand, led to considerable public prejudice against them. Sir George Grey in an historic 'Memorandum on the Immigration of Chinese in the Colony' presented to both Houses of Parliament in 1879, said in what I am sure were carefully chosen words:

> The presence in this country of a large population of Chinese, or of any cognate race, would exercise a deteriorating effect upon its civilisation.

Referring to the fact that there were practically no Chinese women, he added:

> This is a subject which need not be alluded to at length. Those who choose to think it out, and to follow it into its various ramifications, will find it pregnant with interest, and will, I think, be forced to admit that it must prove prolific in disasters to New Zealand.

He referred to the 'struggle which must take place in this part of the world against barbarism', to no possible chance being permitted that the European population should be 'to any extent interfered with by a people of an inferior degree of civilisation', to the future depending 'upon the inhabitants of New Zealand being true to themselves, and preserving uninjured and unmixed that Anglo-Saxon population which now inhabits it, and the pure-bred descendants of which ought to inhabit these islands for all time'.

Yet Grey was no racist. His comments merely echo the sentiments of his day, nauseating and unreal though we may find them. Seddon, liberal though he was, spoke even more forcibly against the Chinese menace.

Special restrictions were placed on their entry, including education tests and a poll tax imposed in 1881 which remained until 1944. The Chinese were an unwanted people. Work for them was confined to menial occupations such as laundering, or eking out an existence in small-scale market gardening where they lived in deplorable housing conditions. Many of them crowded together in the centre of cities, in rows of slum houses often given over to pakapoo gambling or opium smoking. The most opulent were those who sold fruit and vegetables in street stalls or shops.

Today, the Chinese streets where woman would not walk at night, and might not even in the daytime, are gone:

> Recently, new relationships have developed. Many New Zealanders are finding Chinese as their neighbours, fellow-workers in offices and factories, fellow-worshippers in churches, room-mates in hostels, and friends with whom they participate in social activities. This has taken place only in the last decade. . . . Significant changes have taken place in the Chinese community in New Zealand and changes are still taking place. . . . The coming of wives changes their attitude completely. . . . The younger generation, after some years of education in New Zealand schools, speaks more English than Chinese, and has adopted New Zealand ways of life.[15]

This is a New Zealand-Chinese university graduate writing in 1959. And she adds as her opinion: 'The problem of assimilation of any immigrant group is primarily a problem relating to the attitude of the dominant society.'

Limited Chinese immigration has resumed in the last 25 years, particularly of women and families of local Chinese. But the most

---

[15] Fong, N. B. *The Chinese in New Zealand*, Hong Kong University Press, 1959, pp. 2 and 127.

important additions have been by birth in New Zealand. More than half the Chinese have now been born here.

I have covered the position of the Chinese at some length because it demonstrates the changed attitude in New Zealand to people of other races even though—as in the case of these people—they retain substantially their racial integrity, yet are New Zealanders.

Indians

Indians are more recent arrivals than the Chinese. The 4,403 recorded in the 1961 census include 58 percent born out of New Zealand, and three-quarters of these had arrived since the Second World War, some of them from Fiji but most of them from the traditional (indeed almost sole) area of Indian emigration to New Zealand—the area of Gujarat, north of Bombay. There was an earlier burst of Indian migration from there between 1916 and 1921, but with a renewal of anti-Asian prejudice and the introduction of the Immigration Restriction Amendment Act of 1920 the numbers were reduced to a trickle for over 20 years.

The original Gujarati immigrants were peasants from a grossly over-populated area. They were nearly all men and most hoped to take up farming, the few who were artisans such as shoe-makers expecting to be able to continue their trades. But land was too costly to buy, and they were forced into labouring work such as land drainage and scrub cutting, or menial tasks as servants or washermen, or into hawking fruit and vegetables, bottles and rags. They met with occupational prejudice and social rejection which their Hindu religion helped them to accept with impassive stoicism.[16]

Since the end of the war, wives and families have been permitted to come to New Zealand, but this has still confined emigration from India mainly to the one small area. It has, however, created greater stability while social acceptance and occupational distribution have greatly improved. New Zealand-born Indians have increased from 4 percent of the total number in 1936 to 42 percent in 1961.

Indians, like Chinese and Polynesians, tend to be concentrated heavily in Auckland and Wellington, and (like the recent Maori migrants) within the central core of these cities. Indians still have strong if diminishing ties with their homeland, often return or

[16] McGee, T. G. "Indian Settlement in New Zealand 1900-56", *New Zealand Geographer*, Vol. XVIII no. 2, October 1962.

revisit it, and have remained largely tight-knit separate communities, united by origin, language, culture and religion—the principal inhibiting factors in the integration of any minority group. There is another group of Indian migrants which has recently given rise to administrative problems: those who form part of the 230,000 Indians in Fiji. Many who came on visitors' permits, although ostensibly holidaying, worked while they were here. They could earn far more in New Zealand than in Fiji, and indeed did useful work. The numbers concerned increased from about 1,000 permits in 1961 to 5,000 in 1965; when it was time to return they often could not be found, and they were inclined to resort to all kinds of unethical practices in order to stay. Accordingly, the Government found it necessary early in 1967 to suspend permission for this group of visitors to take up employment while in this country.

Polynesians

Polynesians (other than New Zealand Maoris) first arrived in sizeable numbers during the war years, followed by a steady flow in the late 1940s. The rate increased substantially in the next decade, as the following census figures of persons of Polynesian blood reveal: 1951, 3,624; 1961, 14,340. The increase was only partly accounted for by immigration since New Zealand-born Polynesians rose in this period from 1,056 to 5,640. (These figures do not include persons of mixed Polynesian and New Zealand Maori origin who numbered 1,607 in 1961.) Most Polynesians have come from the Cook Islands, Niue Island, Western Samoa and Tonga. In April 1961 over 71 percent were located in Auckland and 17 percent in the Wellington-Hutt area, and being unskilled and semi-skilled only and similar in nature they tend to compete with New Zealand Maoris in the same kind of manual-type occupations and to live under the same kind of urban conditions.

Summary

The following table for selected non-British countries by duration of residence in New Zealand of persons born overseas indicates recency of arrival as at the 1961 census, and also whether they tend to become aggregated in particular areas. An asterisk (*) in the last column means reasonably well dispersed with fairly normal concentration in urban areas.

LENGTH OF RESIDENCE AND PRINCIPAL LOCATION
OF SELECTED GROUPS OF OVERSEAS-BORN

Birthplace	Total No. in New Zealand	Percent with under 15 years' residence	Principal location by statistical areas (for key—see note (3) below)
Denmark	1,715	71.0	*
Germany	2,269	71.6	*; 32% Wgtn.
Austria	950	77.0	50% Wgtn; 21% C. Ak.
Netherlands	17,844	99.5	*; 19% S.A./B.P.
Switzerland	1,099	65.6	34% S.A./B.P. 21% C.Ak.; 18% Tar.; 15% Wgtn.
Latvia	509	91.0	34% Cant.; 28% Wgtn; 21% C.Ak.
Poland	2,140	59.1	56% Wgtn.
Hungary	1,496	95.0	Main cities; 34% Wgtn.
Yugoslavia	3,534	33.2	55% C.Ak.; 14½% both in N'land and Wgtn.
Italy	1,427	50.0	41% Wgtn.
Greece	816	76.0	76% Wgtn.
India	4,753	70.7	44% C.Ak.; 25% Wgtn.
China	4,194	48.5	34% Wgtn.; 30% C.Ak.; 11% Otago.
Western Samoa	4,450	86.8	62% C.Ak.; 21% Wgtn.
Fiji	3,038	71.3	57% C.Ak.; 11% S.A./B.P.; 14% Wgtn.
Cook Islands	3,374	86.9	50% C.Ak.; 17% S.A./B.P.; 22% Wgtn.
Niue Island	1,414	81.9	83% C.Ak.

Notes to Table:

(1) Column 1—Birthplace does not indicate precisely the ethnic group or nationality to which a person belongs. For example, there were 1,330 persons born in Indonesia most of whom were Dutch; from Rumania and Turkey many are Greek; some from India and Malaysia are British; many from Fiji are Indians.

(2) Column 2—The number excludes persons who are born in New Zealand, and therefore must not be taken as the total number of nationals of the origin shown.

(3) Abbreviations used in column 4 for selected statistical areas, with the percentage of total population in each area, are: N'land=Northland (3.6%); C.Ak.=Central Auckland (21.3%); S.A./B.P.=South Auckland/Bay of Plenty (14.5%); Tar.=Taranaki (4.1%); Wgtn= Wellington (19.6%); Cant.=Canterbury (14.3%); Otago=Otago (7.3%). Where statistical areas bear the names of cities they cover a much wider area than the cities concerned.

These figures will have changed quite a little for some countries since 1961. They do help to indicate, however, two things: (1) the degree to which non-British migration was stimulated following the war; (2) a tendency for all nationalities other than northern European to become concentrated in particular localities.

The ratio of mixed blood to full blood in races other than European and Maori is, in conjunction with the information in the previous table, some indication of their capacity to assimilate or integrate with the existing population. Some of the mixture occurred, of course, prior to arrival in New Zealand.

Race or Nationality	Percentage of Mixed Blood to Total
Polynesian—	
Cook Island Maoris	32
Niuean	19
Samoan	55
Other Polynesians	70
Fijians	79
Syrians, Lebanese or Arab	54
Indian	20
Chinese	10
All Other Races	63

The total number of persons (other than Maoris of less than half New Zealand Maori blood) declaring themselves to be of mixed blood was 31,012. The degree of mixed blood is not by any means a complete test of integration. The fairly well-integrated Chinese, for instance, have intermarried with others very little, the less well-integrated Indians twice as much. The high percentage of mixed blood among Fijians is largely accounted for by inter-marriage prior to arrival in New Zealand.

Current policy in non-British migration

Immigration to New Zealand is governed by the Immigration Act 1964, which requires that all persons wishing to enter New Zealand other than returning New Zealand citizens must have an entry permit. This applies to everyone irrespective of race, colour or nationality, including British and Australian citizens. The Act itself does not specifically lay down, however, the policy to be followed in issuing such permits, this being a matter for the Government.

The Government has stated a number of times its basic policy: to admit into New Zealand in *reasonable numbers* those people who

(1) can make an economic or cultural contribution here,

(2) have the capacity to assimilate readily, and

(3) are acceptable to the community generally.

These are broad criteria, and are stated as being for the welfare of the immigrants themselves as well as of the community into which they will settle.

Such matters as age, health, character, occupational skills, cultural background, ethnic origin, marital and family status, and language are deemed to be relevant factors to be taken into account. It must be borne in mind that Government immigration policies have for over a century been closely linked with the provision of occupational skill (and in the earlier years, land development) rather than with broadening the cultural base of the New Zealand people. I pass no judgment on this, but simply state it as a fact.

Policies are not always easy to work out in practice, and in New Zealand the following points bear upon their determination and application:

(1) The number of overseas-born people New Zealand can absorb is governed by the optimum rate of population growth which is possible without disturbing unduly our social and economic structure. Since New Zealand has a fairly high rate of natural increase, its relative *need* for immigrants is less than for countries like Australia or Canada if it wishes to achieve the same rate of population growth.

(2) The introduction of people from overseas, especially non-Europeans, must be determined with proper regard for the fact that we already have a multi-racial society, and with it a special duty to the Maori people and the internal migratory problems they present.

(3) New Zealand accepts that it has special obligations to Cook Islanders. Niueans, Tokelauans (all of whom are New Zealand citizens) and to residents of Western Samoa with which it has had in the past a trustee relationship. Upwards of 2,000 persons from these territories are admitted annually. Clearly their admission reduces the opportunities than can be offered to people from other parts of the world.

(4) The majority of New Zealanders are of British stock. English is the language spoken, British institutions and law and customs form the background of our society; therefore people of British descent fit most smoothly into our life and are most likely to have the type of education and skills to fit them occupationally to meet our needs.

(5) A large number of people from the British Isles and Australia come here 'under their own steam' to settle. Most of the rest of our permanent intake is brought under Government-aided or sponsored schemes to meet labour shortages of specific kinds. The most suitable people for this purpose have proved to be British, together with some other Europeans. (Assisted immigrants make up only one-eighth of our permanent arrivals.)

(6) New Zealand, in consequence of its greater participation in international affairs, has increased its obligations in the field of international migration, e.g. to accept refugees.

Comparisons with Australia

New Zealand's immigration policies, especially in relation to non-British Europeans, are sometimes contrasted unfavourably with Australia's. The following points should be borne in mind:

(1) Population increase January 1951 to December 1964— Australia 35.4 percent, New Zealand 36.3 percent.

(2) To achieve almost the same rate of population increase as New Zealand, Australia has been forced into a more active and less selective policy of immigration from European sources. The percentage of overseas-born people in the Australian population was well below New Zealand's until 1954. In 1961 it was higher at 16.9 compared with 14.0

(3) Australia's rate of increase in overseas-born nationals slowed down markedly after the initial postwar burst. In the period 1947-54 the average rate was 8.14 percent; in the next seven years, 4.74 percent.

(4) Australia has received since the war much larger *pro rata* gains in population from Germany, Greece, Italy, Malta and other European countries than New Zealand. On the other hand, New Zealand's gains from non-European sources, especially Asia and the Pacific, have been higher than Australia's. In 1964 there were more than 30,000

people (0.3 percent of the population) in Australia other than Europeans or aboriginals.[17] Some 12,000 were Asian or other students, and 8,000 admitted for temporary residence. Our numbers in New Zealand other than Europeans and Maoris at the 1961 census exceeded the Austtralian total, and represented proportionately more than four times as many.

(5) Another important difference is in the indigenous populations. Aboriginals and Torres Islanders in Australia in June 1961 numbered 84,470, or 0.8 percent of the population. The indigenous Maori population of New Zealand at almost the same date was 167,086 or 6.9 percent of the total.

(6) The non-European population of New Zealand in 1961 was proportionately more than seven times as great as that of Australia. However, in view of the disparity in population from non-British European sources it may be fairer to compare persons of non-British stock in the two countries. In round figures the proportions are 9 percent for Australia and 12 percent for New Zealand.

All that these points really prove is that a country's policy in regard to immigration which will result in minority groups and racial admixtures must be geared to its needs. Australia's policy is substantially based on population growth, in the first instance implemented for defence purposes, with economic reasons added later. New Zealand's policy is based mainly on labour requirements.

A 'White New Zealand' policy?

So long as we can achieve a satisfactory rate of population growth, there seems no need to look for immigrants far beyond people of British descent who want to come here, and those from the Pacific Islands for which we accept a moral responsibility. However, as a result of this circumstance it appears to some people that New Zealand is actually discriminating against non-Europeans and even against some Europeans. They say that this policy is 'rationalised' by the politicians on the grounds that New Zealand is a small country, too small to afford to accept immigrants who cannot readily be assimilated culturally, and who tend to form isolated communities within but apart from the main

[17] Official Year Book of the Commonwealth of Australia, No. 50, 1964, p. 304.

body of the population. The fact remains, however, that we cannot afford immigrants who offer us little in skills and plenty in headaches and who, as additions to our current intake, might well force our rate of population growth to levels where inflation would become even harder to control.

Many advocates of a more liberal Asian or African immigration policy infer that, in saying that such groups are more difficult culturally and socially to integrate or assimilate, the Government is saying something about the colour of their skin. There are some people admittedly who confuse a reason with a prejudice, but the Government has declared itself as being concerned with one 'c' and not the other—with culture (and associated factors) and not with colour. Whatever may have been the attitude in the Victorian era of patronising colonialism, few reasonable people in New Zealand now believe in discrimination against Asians on the sole grounds of ethnic origin.

It must also be said that practically no country in the world today has a policy of unrestricted entry or unqualified asylum. Indeed, it is not always realised that some countries whose nationals we are sometimes accused of excluding on grounds of colour or origin, themselves provide almost impenetrable barriers to the entry of persons of many other races. We are living in a day when it seems that European peoples are becoming more tolerant, and many non-European peoples more exclusive.

Isolated instances of the application of New Zealand government policy to indivdual persons of others races have seemed to some people to amount to unfair discrimination or a 'White New Zealand' policy. Rarely are people in possession of all the facts from which to make an informed judgment, and often for very good reasons these facts cannot be given to them. The general accusation should be seen, however, in the light of the two following items:

* 25 percent of all permanent entry permits to New Zealand are to persons of non-European or only part-European origin;
* between the 1956 and 1961 censuses the European population in New Zealand increased by 10 percent, the Maori population by 22 percent, and the 'Other Races' by 50 percent.

That New Zealand adopts a reasonably liberal policy toward the entry of persons other than those of British nationality is shown by the following figures concerning the result of entry applications by such persons for the year ended 31 March 1965:

Category	Number of Persons Involved	
	Approved	Declined
Permanent entry	1,752	2,908
Temporary entry	2,184	419
Student permits	272	193
Extension of temporary permits	2,813	167
Extension of student permits	394	16
Re-entry permits	2,592	57
Permanent residence	774	85
Totals	10,781	3,845

Applications were declined because the persons concerned were not able to provide evidence that they could support themselves or meet the minimum criteria for granting permits. Applications were received from persons of 90 nationalities and countries of origin and granted in respect of 88, persons from Africa and naturalised British being counted as one group each. The applications were 90 percent higher than three years earlier, when they related to only 55 nationalities or countries of origin.

Many applications are granted which do not strictly satisfy the normal criteria; in fact, about 20 percent of issued permits are to people who although not conforming with the criteria, are admitted on humanitarian and similar grounds. This allows many Pacific Islanders, Chinese, Indians and others to strengthen their communities or complete their family units, it also permits the acceptance of numbers of refugees each year, and it enables sympathetic consideration to be given to applications from part-Europeans, whose position in parts of the world which are becoming more nationalistic is often not easy.

Further evidence of a liberal policy is found in New Zealand's admission of quite considerable numbers of foreign students at a time when our educational facilities are being taxed to the full to accommodate the fast-rising demands of our own population. At 30 September 1965 there were 931 overseas private students studying in New Zealand from 25 countries or territories, mainly from Asia and the Pacific, as well as 556 Colombo Plan students from 17 countries, 92 scholars under the Special Commonwealth Assistance to Africa Plan (SCAAP), 130 Commonwealth Education Scholars (CES), and 90 Samoan students under special scholarships. Since one of the main purposes in admitting overseas students is to enable them to use the higher education they obtain to benefit their own people, they are admitted for limited periods only.

Where are we going?

Future trends in birthrates, which are always susceptible to unanticipated influences, have recently become even more unpredictable. Other factors in the nature of population growth such as migration and inter-racial marriage can be predicted only by using assumptions which future events may invalidate. Therefore, to predict the future is a most uncertain exercise, at best—a kind of 'informed guess'. Looking ahead 25 years the Government Statistician has projected on one set of assumptions a total population in 1990 of 4,784,000. It seems likely that some 500,000 of these will be census-classified Maoris, making up by then more than 10 percent of the population. (Ten years further ahead at the turn of the century there will be another 200,000 to be counted.) In addition, by 1990 there may well be another 500,000 persons of part (but less than half) Maori blood. The Polynesian population of Pacific origin or stock will probably be increased substantially, but by how much is anybody's guess. It is certain, however, that this group will continue to intermingle and marry with New Zealand Maoris and that the national origins will become increasingly blurred. The preponderance of the younger ages in these two groups will lessen and they will increasingly contribute to the working population. Indeed, their absorption into employment in a world where higher skills and education will be demanded will be a considerable challenge.

I believe that, despite the need for increased agricultural production, for exploitation of our natural resources, and for the industrial development of areas other than the principal cities, the so-called 'drift' from rural to urban areas is irreversible. The consequent movement of large numbers of young persons into cities and towns, and especially those of non-European race, will impose new strains upon community resources and upon human behaviour and attitudes.

Immigration from traditional sources will probably flow very much as in the past without any substantial change in the kinds of countries from which we shall receive our intake. New Zealand ethnically will still be substantially European, yet rather less so than now, in consequence of the increased Maori and Polynesian populations, and of more frequent intermarriage between races. Our way of life will continue to be based on British institutions and ideologies, but modified increasingly to meet the requirements of a changing population structure and of the role we may expect to play in the Pacific and South-East Asia.

Alternative Policy Patterns in Multi-racial Societies

A. JOAN METGE

Since words are their principal tools, social scientists find it necessary to give them precision by careful definition. Before I begin to examine the alternative policy patterns of multi-racial societies, I think it would be helpful to define the way in which I shall be using certain words.

Race

In popular use, *race* is employed vaguely and ambiguously for a wide variety of groups and categories held together by many different kinds of bonds: not only by hereditary physical features (e.g. the Negroid, Mongoloid and Caucasoid races), but also by religion (Hindus, Jews), common culture and traditions (British, Scots), or a combination of hereditary physical type, history and citizenship (the American Negro). Using the term thus imprecisely both reflects and encourages the assumption that there is a genetic connection between physical traits and cultural ones. In fact, however, this is demonstrably not the case: physical type, language and culture often vary independently. Scientists generally agree that the word *race* should be used primarily in a bio-physical sense, to describe 'a sub-group of peoples possessing a definite combination of physical characters of genetic origin'.[1] Technically speaking, many groups commonly described as races are not races at all—the Maori, for instance, and the British.

Even in this sense, races are not 'real things' that man has discovered, but sets of categories which he has constructed. These categories are based, it is true, on clusters of hereditary physical characteristics—stature, skin colour, head form, shape and colour of eyes, colour and texture of hair, shape of nose, etc.—but the clusters do not form discrete and invariable entities. In the first place, few such characteristics divide people into clear-cut exclusive groups (as blood-types do): most of them present a gradual, continuous variation, for instance from very pale to very dark in skin colour, and from narrow to round in head shape. Second, they are not fixed for all time, but are continually changing in response to environmental influences and human manipulation. And third, they vary independently of each other, so that a narrow nose (for instance) can occur with any gradation of skin colour or hair texture. Thus the classification of races even in purely biological terms is fraught with difficulties: no classification yet proposed has won universal acceptance. One thing is clear: there are no pure races, and no unchanging ones. There is a lot to be said for the view that there is only one race—the human race.

Some social scientists accept the use of word *race* in a social as well as a biological sense as long as it is realised that there is a difference. Bohannan, for instance, defines *race* as 'socially recognised categories into which people are thrust on the basis of socially recognised physiological criteria'.[2]

Other sociologists always put the word in quotation marks when using it to refer to socially defined groups, or speak of the 'so-called races'. But many scientists prefer to restrict the term to its biological sense, and use other terms such as *ethnic group* or *minority*.

The term *ethnic group* is used to designate a group of persons bound together by common origin and interests, sometimes but not always distinguished by certain hereditary physical features, sometimes but not always possessing a distinctive culture, and characterised by a consciousness of kind, a we-feeling. The term

[1] Krogman, W.M.: 'The Concept of Race', *The Science of Man in the World Crisis, ed.* Ralph Linton, Columbia University Press, N.Y. 1940, p. 49.

[2] Bohannan, Paul: *Social Anthropology,* Holt, Rinehart, and Winston, 1963, p. 198.

is in fact a very flexible one which can be used to cover groups of several different types.

Minority means literally 'the smaller number'. Some sociologists, however, have divested it of all statistical meaning, and redefined it as 'a group of people who, because of physical or cultural characteristics, are singled out from the others in the society in which they live for differential and unequal treatment, and who therefore regard themselves as objects of collective discrimination'.[3] I personally prefer to use *minority* to mean a group of people distinguished by certain common characteristics but smaller in size than the largest comparable group in the society, and generally find *ethnic group* the more useful term.

Race relations

The word *race* is also frequently used in a number of compounds—race differences, race relations, race problems, race prejudice, and in the terms of our title, multi-racial society. In some cases, these terms really do refer to the biological races, but most often they are concerned with what I have called ethnic groups and the relations between them. To substitute *ethnic group* for *race* in these compounds is impossibly clumsy. Some sociologists prefer to talk of 'intergroup relations' and 'group prejudice', but such terms fail to suggest the real issue. The alternative usually suggested for 'multiracial society' is 'plural society', but this term suggests a society in which pluralism—i.e. a degree of voluntary separate development—not only exists but is accepted as right and proper. We can, I think, justify using terms like *race relations* and *multi-racial society* on the grounds of word economy and general acceptance, but we must not lose sight of the fact that we are referring to groups defined by a combination of biological and social characteristics, and not to purely biological divisions.

Group membership

Individuals become members of ethnic groups by descent, that is, through their parents. This is entirely automatic when both parents belong to the same group, but there is quite a variety of ways of handling the problem of affiliation when they do not. Sometimes those of mixed descent are rejected by both parents' groups and assigned to a third and separate one; sometimes the

---

3 Wirth, Louis: 'The Problem of Minority Groups', *The Science of Man in the World Crisis*, op. cit., p. 347.

socially dominant group assigns them all to the other group, sometimes only those who are 'half or more' or those who are physically identifiable. Or a self-conscious minority may claim anyone descended from a member and who desires membership. It is however, comparatively rare for individuals to be left entirely free to make their own identification. Most societies have some basic principle which they apply in this situation.

In the case of the New Zealand Maoris, there is no standard legal definition—a fact for which we can be duly grateful. Some laws define a Maori as 'a person belonging to the aboriginal race of New Zealand, including a half-caste and a person intermediate between a half-caste and a person of pure descent from that race'; others extend the definition to include 'any descendant of a Maori as otherwise defined' as a Maori for their purposes. The Statistics Department counts in the Maori population 'all Maoris of full blood, all persons with half or more Maori blood and all mixtures of Maoris with Other Polynesians'.[4] This count is based on declarations made on census schedules in answer to a question about 'degree of Maori blood'.

The concept of 'Maori blood' derives from an ancient and widespread belief that blood is the linking factor in kinship and the carrier of physical and personality characteristics. Scientifically, it is quite invalid: inherited characteristics are transmitted not 'in the blood' but by the genes, and the distribution of blood types cuts right across ethnic groups, though there is variation in the relative frequency of their occurrence. From the social and psychological point of view, this concept of 'blood' is dangerous, since it encourages the description of individuals as *half-castes* or *half-bloods,* as if they were less than whole men, and fosters the emotional belief that when 'the bloods' are 'mixed' (as a result of intermarriage), one is diluted or polluted by the other.

The problem of terminology can be simply resolved by recognising that what we are talking about is not physical heredity but *ancestry* and *social identification.* The fractions in which 'degrees of Maori blood' are normally stated express not an analysis of blood content but the proportion of Maoris to pakehas in a person's ancestry. Such a fraction is worked out by tracing his

4 Statistics Department: *New Zealand Census 1961,* Vol. 8, 'Maori Population and Dwellings', Government Printer, Wellington, p. 16.

ancestry back to the earliest generation in which a pakeha figures and then reckoning the proportion of Maori to pakeha ancestors in that and subsequent generations.

It would not be difficult to prove that in a large number of cases the fractions declared on census schedules are not objectively accurate. Sometimes the inaccuracy is due to ignorance of all the relevant facts. (How many pakehas could trace their ancestry back the six to eight generations necessary to cover the period in which a pakeha ancestor is a possibility for most Maoris?) Sometimes it is due to mistakes in arithmetic. But in many if not most cases, what are mis-statements judged as objective measures of ancestry are subjectively accurate statements of social identification. For most of those involved, the fraction asked for has no meaning: the real issue for them is whether they align themselves with the Maori social group or the pakeha one. If the latter, they frequently understate their degree of Maori ancestry, even ignoring it entirely if it is small. If the former, they frequently overstate it, not only to bring them within the census definition of a Maori as a person who is 'half Maori or more', but often to assert themselves as 'full Maori' because that is the way they feel, in spite of one or even several pakeha ancestors.

In societies comprising two or more ethnic groups, social identification—whether freely chosen or imposed from outside—matters far more than the objective facts of ancestry. Though in an unintended fashion, the census gives us in its count of 'the Maori population' a truly useful measure of the Maori social group.

Culture

The term 'culture' is popularly used with a capital C to refer to 'the arts', a certain set of intellectual and aesthetic activities. We New Zealanders often complain that we have 'no culture of our own', meaning nothing obviously different from the culture of the country from which most of our ancestors originally came. When we talk about 'Maori culture' we usually mean either the arts and crafts that are immediately recognisable as Maori or those customs, institutions, ideas and arts and crafts which can be shown to have their origin in pre-European Maori society. But sociologists give the word a much wider meaning. As one famous definition puts it: 'Culture is that complex whole which includes knowledge, belief, art, morals, law, custom and any other capabilities and habits acquired by man as a member of society'.[5] It is, in short, a people's whole way of life. New Zealanders do have a culture in this sense, even if it is not markedly different from that of other countries of British origin. 'Maori culture' is the way Maoris live today, not just what has survived from their pre-European past.

Where ethnic groups have been in contact for some time, as Maoris and pakehas have, within the framework of one state, they usually come to share a considerable area of cultural experience. Cultures are never exclusive, discrete entities, but overlap to a lesser or greater extent. Whether any two groups are described as having separate cultures or whether they are seen as distinctive variations on a single basic culture depends largely on the attitude of the describer.

It is perhaps necessary to remind ourselves that cultures do not have a life of their own. It is tempting to talk about a 'meeting of cultures' or the 'clash of cultures', but in fact it is not cultures which meet or clash but people—the many individuals who are the carriers of their respective cultures.

The range of variation

The factors involved in relations between different ethnic groups within the framework of a single state are so numerous and various that in each country the situation is unique, and the making of generalisations is accordingly hazardous. In no two instances have those interrelations followed exactly the same pattern. However, wherever ethnic groups do meet within the same society it can be confidently predicted that there will be, at least to some degree, conflict, biological mixing, acculturation (or interchange of cultural elements, however uneven), attempts at domination, and reactions against it.

The variety of situations possible can be simplified a little by distinguishing three types:

(1) Societies with inhabitants of different racial stock but the same culture (e.g. Negro and European in U.S.A.).

(2) Societies with inhabitants of the same racial stock but different cultures (e.g. English and French in Canada).

(3) Societies with inhabitants of different racial stock and different cultures.

---

[5] Tylor, Edward B.: *Primitive Culture*, 3rd ed,. John Murray, London, 1891, p. 1.

Policy and process

Mention of 'policy patterns in multi-racial societies' immediately calls to mind at least three words: segregation, assimilation, integration. Sociologists would add two other theoretical possibilities: pluralism and fusion.

In discussing these alternatives, we immediately come up against two problems. First, every one of these words can be used in different ways. They may describe official policy, or alternatively what is actually happening. All except pluralism can be used to refer to a process, and all five can be used to describe the condition which is the end result of that process. As policies, segregation, assimilation, integration and fusion are concerned with achievement of this final state, the completion of the process. Any stage short of the final state should properly be described as partial or incomplete segregation, assimilation, integration or fusion, as the case may be.

Second, it is much easier to find out what has happened and is happening in other countries than to find out what the official policy is. I had originally intended to describe the policy patterns and then the actual state of intergroup relations of certain countries, notably South Africa, the continental U.S.A., Hawaii, Fiji, Brazil. But while there was no difficulty about obtaining detailed descriptions of the state of intergroup relations in these countries, I found it impossible to get reliable statements of their policy, except in the case of South Africa. For one thing, many governments seem to have different policies for different groups (e.g. the U.S.A.). For another, policies frequently change over time. In the U.S.A., for instance, the Government's Indian policy was for many years based on the assumption that the Indians were a 'vanishing race'. Then it shifted to a policy of isolation and segregation, when Indians were confined to reservations. Later the emphasis changed to forced assimilation and steps were taken to 'civilise' the Indians and 'integrate' them into American society. More recently, doubts as to the justice, desirability and practicability of compulsory assimilation have led to a policy involving the fostering and perpetuating of many features of Indian culture.

Because of these problems I had to abandon my original plan. Instead I propose to discuss the possible alternatives in general terms, drawing examples where I can from a variety of countries.

Segregation

The dictionary meaning of 'to segregate' is 'to separate, isolate, put aside from the rest'. Some sociologists distinguish between voluntary and involuntary segregation, but most classify voluntary separation—whether by mutual consent or through the unforced withdrawal of one group from the rest—as pluralism, and restrict segregation to involuntary separation, imposed by a dominant group upon itself and the other ethnic groups in the society, through its control of economic wealth and governmental functions.

As a policy, segregation is concerned to keep certain ethnic groups (not necessarily all that are present) separate, unmixed, and ranked in a hierarchy. To this end, administrators use both formal and informal sanctions to limit contact, communication, and other social relations.

Segregation operates under a variety of circumstances and assumes a multitude of forms: not only apartheid, but Chinatown, the Jewish ghetto, and the Jim Crow-ism of the southern states of the U.S.A. There are wide variations in the extent to which it is embodied in legislation, but it is always supported by law, indirectly if not directly.

Segregation circumscribes the choices of all citizens to some extent in most if not all the fields of residence, education, employment, marriage, recreation, and political participation, but in particular it limits the rights of members of certain ethnic groups in comparison with members of the dominant group, placing an absolute bar across their upward mobility. Segregation invariably involves an unequal distribution of wealth, privilege, and responsibility, and the stratification of the total society on the basis of ethnic group membership.

Taken to its logical conclusion, segregation requires complete physical separation: this is the ultimate aim of apartheid. However, social distance can be effectively maintained without physical separation. Custom and tradition may erect barriers between groups which isolate them as effectively as stone walls or miles of open space. In the Guatemalan town of San Louis Jilotepeque, Indians and *Ladinos* live side by side all over town, and are so interdependent that they could not live without each other. But custom so limits their social intercourse that the two groups have virtually different civilisations. In the southern states of the U.S.A., physical contacts between Negroes and whites are numerous and frequent, and residential segregation not pronounced. But until recently custom decreed that they attend different churches and schools, forbad their eating or drinking or participating in recreation together, and even regulated such behaviour as conversation, sitting and standing in each other's presence, use of titles, and bodily posture. Members of a group regarded as inferior can always be admitted to the company of their 'superiors' provided they display the signs of inferiority—the waiter's white jacket, and deferential form of address.

Segregation is sometimes considered necessary to protect members of a primitive group from disease or the disorganising impact of modern civilisation, e.g. the Canadian Government in relation to Indians of the offshore islands of British Columbia, Denmark with regard to the Greenland Eskimo. But the most common reasons underlying adoption of a policy of segregation—whether admitted or not—are to preserve the purity of stock and the superior socio-economic status of the dominant group, to control potential competitors, and to facilitate or excuse exploitation. It is usually associated with a deeply rooted belief in the inherent superiority of the stock and culture of the dominant group, and in the inferiority of the others.

Assimilation

According to the dictionary 'to assimilate' can be used as a transitive verb to mean 'to make similar, to absorb into the system', or as an intransitive verb, to mean 'to be so absorbed'. Assimilation is most commonly adopted as a policy in societies where the group which is dominant in culture and political power is also dominant in numbers. It aims to produce a homogeneous society, by getting members of minority groups to discard their culture in favour of that of the dominant one. By those involved it is generally perceived as a one-way process. 'Assimilation means your total absorption into my culture.' 'Assimilation is what the shark said to the kahawai before he opened his mouth and swallowed him for breakfast.' In practice, assimilation is not completely one-sided. The dominant group acquires something as a result of contact with the minority, even if only a few words and recipes. But undoubtedly one group sets the pattern, into which the other is required to fit.

On the face of it, assimilation would seem to be the polar opposite of segregation, because the dominant group is willing to accept members of other ethnic groups as equals; but this willingness is contingent on their accepting its culture. Equal treatment has to be earned. Assimilation is like segregation in being firmly based on a belief in the superiority of the dominant culture.

The process of assimilation is by no means automatic, and is subject to many delays and setbacks. Even under the most favourable circumstances it takes at least two or three generations. An individual who is reared in one society and has acquired its culture cannot in a single lifetime completely divest himself of all that he has learned and take up a completely new set of customs, skills, beliefs and values, and perhaps a new language. The rate and smoothness of assimilation depend on a whole variety of factors: relative numbers, the attitudes of members of the dominant group, the attitudes of members of the minority group(s), the similarity or dissimilarity of their cultures, the extent and nature of physical differences (especially any difference in colour), the manner and rate of entrance of the minorities into the country, relative distribution (especially between urban and rural areas), the influence of personalities on both sides. Assimilation is smooth and rapid only when members of the minority group themselves have strong motives for wishing to be assimilated—and even then, only if there are no barriers to their absorption, such as pride in ancestry on the part of members of the dominant group, or their own distinctive skin colour which gives them high visibility in the population, no matter how much they may think and act like everyone else.

Minority groups have undoubtedly been fully assimilated in various countries at various time, but it is difficult to think of examples, because by definition the groups concerned have vanished without trace. Achievement of the final state of complete assimilation would seem to be achieved most often when assimilation is not made official policy. Official adoption seems invariably to arouse reaction and resistance.

Prior to the First World War, the U.S.A. followed a *laissez faire* policy toward the various ethnic groups migrating across the Atlantic from Europe. American society was regarded as a great 'melting-pot' and it was taken for granted that immigrants would be assimilated quickly and painlessly. This comfortable belief received a rude shock during the First World War, when the nation, taking stock of itself, found that millions of its inhabitants could neither read, speak, nor write the English language, that less than half the foreign-born white males of voting age had become citizens, that immigrants were concentrated in 'colonies' in the cities, and that some immigrants were being encouraged by foreign governments to maintain their old allegiance.

As a result of these revelations an Americanisation Movement was officially launched. Deliberate organised efforts were made to divest the immigrant of his foreign heritage, to teach him English, and to inject into him a loyalty to American institutions. The movement used many agencies: public schools, patriotic societies, chambers of commerce, women's clubs, public libraries, and industrial firms. But the Americanisation Movement succeeded no better than the earlier policy. Because it assumed that American culture was a finished product in an Anglo-Saxon pattern, devalued minority cultures, and involved varying degrees of coercion and suppression, it aroused the resentment of those at whom it was directed, and ultimately defeated its purpose.

Over and over again, active assimilation programmes have given rise not only to resistance, but to reactive adaptation, involving withdrawal from both physical and cultural contact, the elaboration and glorification of the threatened culture, and sometimes the emergence of nativistic cults aimed at reaffirming the value of the minority group and its ways.

Even when they have a positive attitude towards change, people do not discard their culture or even parts of it like an old garment, all at once or without repercussions. They borrow selectively, beginning with material goods and only gradually extending their interest to ideas, institutions, beliefs and values. Moreover, instead of dropping an element of their own heritage and replacing it neatly and completely with a new one they usually modify their own ways to fit the new environment and modify what they borrow to suit their needs—a process known as progressive adaptation. In this way they may retain a distinctive cultural identity for a considerable length of time, though moving appreciably closer to the dominant culture. Of all the nations who have pursued a policy of assimilation over the last century or two, remarkably few have seen it through to its conclusion; most still contain minority groups in various stages of assimilation, changing at widely varying rates.

Pluralism

Pluralism is also known as symbiosis or cultural democracy. Symbiosis is properly a biological term used to describe a permanent union between organisms which are distinct but depend for their existence on each other. As a policy, pluralism aims to unite different ethnic groups in a relationship of mutual interdependence, respect and equality, while permitting them to maintain and cultivate their distinctive ways. It may involve physical separation but most often does not. Whatever separation exists is voluntarily chosen, not imposed. Whatever lines of cleavage there are are vertical ones: ideally there should be no ranking of one group above the other. Pluralism 'implies cooperation rather than conflict between majority and minority groups, appreciation of the cultural heritages of minorities, preservation and incorporation of some of (their) . . . elements rather than complete repression, and realization that modification must take place slowly in order to avoid cultural disintegration and social maladjustment. . . .'[6] Certain limits must, however, be placed on cultural freedom: the privilege of in-group nurture must always be subordinated to allegiance to the nation.

Pluralism may be regarded as a more or less permanent arrangement (stabilised pluralism) or as a temporary measure 'to avoid cultural disintegration and social maladjustment'.

Societies attempting to put this policy into practice run into certain difficulties. Equality and interdependence between the constituent ethnic groups are hard to maintain when these groups are unequal in numbers, economic wealth, political power and prestige, or when their value systems differ radically. Allowing ethnic groups to maintain different methods of internal political organisation and property ownership can lead to situations where, though the groups may in theory be equal, their members in practice are not, because they do not have the same rights. (This is the situation in Fiji between Fijians, Indians, and Europeans.) It is one thing for the State to permit the groups themselves to raise barriers to free mixing, but such barriers cannot be embodied in legislation without imposing segregation. Pluralism is in constant danger of developing into ethnic stratification. By endorsing voluntary separation and the cultivation of differences, it encourages the development of group stereotypes and the prejudging of individuals on the basis of group membership.

Few societies have managed to avoid all the pitfalls. Perhaps Switzerland comes closest to combining diverse ethnic groups (French, German, Italian and Romansch-speaking) in harmony

---

[6] Davie, M. R. *One America,* ed. Brown and Roucek, Prentice-Hall, 1945, pp. 550-1.

and equality with a high degree of national feeling; and the English, Welsh, and Scots manage to coexist reasonably amicably; but in both cases the groups involved are of basically the same physical stock. Pluralism presents greater problems where cultural differences are more marked, or where there are differences in physical type, as in Canada, Fiji, Malaysia, and Mauritius.

Integration

According to the dictionary, 'to integrate' means 'to combine parts into a whole, to make one'. Integration can accordingly be defined as the process by which diverse parts are combined into a unity, and the condition in which they are so related. Such unification does not entail an insistence on uniformity, that is, the elimination of *all* differences between parts, but only the removal of those differences which disturb or inhibit the total unity. Nor does it imply (in the common phrase) the integration of a minority group and its culture into the majority or dominant one, but rather the integration of two or more groups and their cultures within a single framework.

As a policy, integration has two major aims: the elimination of all purely ethnic lines of cleavage, and the guaranteeing of the same rights, opportunities and responsibilities to all citizens, whatever their group membership. Those who adopt such a policy are therefore committed to acting, by legislation if necessary, to remove all barriers to contact, communication and social relations between groups, to eliminate discrimination and exploitation, and to abolish all circumstances that impose separation or limit rights solely on ethnic grounds. To do this, it may be necessary to provide special assistance to help members of certain groups overcome handicaps, but such measures must be regarded as temporary, as means to an end.

What does integration have to say about cultural differences? Once inequalities have been redressed and barriers to mixing removed, it could be argued that administrators have done all they can or should do, and that they should then leave it to the people themselves to decide the extent to which they do in fact meet, communicate, mix, intermarry, and borrow culturally from each other. In practice, however, government officials find themselves called upon to make a host of practical decisions which presuppose some ideas about the relative value of the cultures involved and the desirability of maintaining or modifying them: decisions for instance about the location of State-financed houses for members of minority groups, about educational programmes, and about State aid for cultural projects. A refusal to allow the teaching of the languages, history and arts of minority groups in State schools, to train teachers in these subjects, or to give financial assistance to minority cultural projects, can amount to applying pressure on minority groups to make them relinquish their own ways. It is clearly desirable that the principles on which decisions are made on such issues should be carefully thought out at the policy level and not merely decided *ad hoc* by junior administrators.

Even when these principles have been formulated, major problems will remain to be solved in putting them into practice. Should the Government refrain entirely from interfering in people's cultural choices? A sound case can be made for remedial action if the choices made lead to increased social distance, stereotyping, and the development of informal sanctions against mixing. But should the Government itself initiate schemes to promote mixing and borrowing on the one hand, or the maintenance of minority ways on the other? How is discrimination to be defined? Is it better dealt with by legislation or by informal sanctions? Who should decide when special measures to help a minority overcome disadvantages and handicaps cease to be compensatory and become discriminatory against other groups? What should be done when the members of a minority prefer inequality to change or oppose the repeal of a law that discriminates against them rather than lose the compensatory privilege associated with it? Does equality of citizenship include the right not only to be different but to be less equal if one chooses? Should the Government act to mitigate the pressures towards assimilation exerted informally by members of the dominant group?

It is also important to demonstrate clearly, in practice as well as in theory, that integration differs from assimilation. Many Maoris resist, or are at best lukewarm in their support of, the policy of integration adopted by the New Zealand Government in the early 1960s because they suspect that 'it is only another name for assimilation'. To change the name without changing the policy is just asking for trouble, for the people concerned are not fooled, and the usefulness of the term is negated.

In contrast to assimilation, a policy of integration implies consciously refraining from bringing pressure to bear on minority groups to abandon their culture. It could be argued that it should go further than this and actively protect minorities from such pressures, since integration is committed to guaranteeing equal rights to all citizens, including the right to be different within the limits of law and order set by an elected legislature. Under a policy of assimilation, members of minority groups are guaranteed equal rights provided that they conform to standards set by the dominant group; integration insists that all citizens are entitled to the same rights unconditionally.

Many administrators seem to assume, implicitly if not explicitly, that integration as a condition can be no more than a stage along the road to eventual assimilation, and hence that a policy of integration is essentially a short-term one, which it may be wise to adopt for the present, but which will sooner or later be outdated by inevitable social processes. But as we have seen, assimilation is by no means inevitable. There are at least two other ways of regarding integration. Like pluralism, integration can be regarded as a condition that is permanently desirable, as a goal in its own right. When this view is held, a policy of integration is a long-term one, aimed at creating and maintaining a fully integrated society in which all citizens share a common basic culture and equal rights and duties, but sections maintain a limited range of distinctive ways. Alternatively, integration can be regarded as a short-term policy leading eventually not to assimilation but to the fusion of cultures.

Fusion

Fusion is the process by which two or more cultures combine to produce another, which is significantly different from each of the parent cultures but includes elements from all of them, together with new ones produced through the stimulation of contact and subsequent internal development. Fusion is complex and many-sided where assimilation is essentially one-sided.

Like assimilation the word fusion can be used to describe both process—at any stage of which it is incomplete or partially achieved—and an end condition. Hawaii and Brazil are countries which are well advanced along the road to fusion, though they have by no means yet achieved it fully. Like assimilation also, fusion can be held up by reluctance on the part of one or more of the groups involved to lose their identity (what Bohannan calls 'cultural narcissism').

Fusion is hardly ever put forward as a policy or a blueprint for immediate action. It is a complex process which nobody seems to be aware of until it is virtually completed. It is most likely to occur in states where there is a large number of ethnic groups, and especially where they are roughly equal in size, prestige, and wealth or where advantages in one direction (such as economic power) are offset by disadvantages (such as limited number) in another. It sometimes happens even when the official policy is one of assimilation, either because of the strength of the minority culture or the adaptability and liberality of the dominant society.

Fusion has the advantage of arousing far less resentment in minority groups than assimilation, because it assigns a value to their culture and promises that it will not be entirely lost. But it is not something that can be forced or hurried: it must develop naturally. It seems to me to be essentially a long term goal to be kept in mind by policy makers who have adopted integration as their immediate goal.

Education's Impact on the Multi-racial Society

R. L. BRADLY

This chapter could almost as aptly have been given the reverse title 'The Multi-Racial Society's Impact on Education' for there are many ways in which New Zealand's mixed society has affected and brought about changes in our educational system. In some cases this influence is obvious; in others it is more subtle.

The early settlers established educational institutions, forms of organisation and classification, and curricula patterned closely on those of the Old Country. It was not long, however, before the system had to be modified to meet the needs and challenges of a different kind of society and, in the years that followed, its influence (especially that of the Maori section) has continued to bring about changes in our educational thought and practice.

The most obvious effects of this influence are those connected with the curriculum. A brief comment on one or two aspects will illustrate the point. Our latest basic infant readers have been designed with Maori interests and word usage in mind, and include stories of Maori life and customs with Maori boys and girls appearing as the central figures; history and social studies syllabuses include large sections relating to the Maori; textbooks and pamphlets have been published by the Education Department on the art of the Maori, and Maori art and craft occupies a prominent place in almost all school timetables; Maori action songs and

Maori games are taught to Maori and pakeha children alike; a Maori Language Committee has been operating for several years and has produced teaching textbooks and bulletins in the Maori language which is now taught wherever it is required in secondary schools. The universities have had to make changes too, and have felt impelled to add Maori studies and Maori language to their degree courses, while the new Waikato University proposes to set up a Maori Research Centre.

Technical Institutes have also been affected and have added special training courses for Maori youths in carpentry, plumbing, electrical wiring and automotive engineering. It is doubtful if any of these courses would have been organised if it had not been apparent that many Maori youths were not continuing with academic careers in which their prospects of success often appeared so limited, and were more interested in practical occupations. As Mr Mardle pointed out in a previous chapter: whether Maori or pakeha, children from homes of manual workers tend to respond to concrete, tangible, immediate and particularised values rather than those that are abstract, intangible or future. They seek for active, open-air types of work rather than sedentary indoor jobs, and for practical work using their hands, strength or manipulative skill rather than physically inactive mental work.

In many less obvious ways too, the influence of the Maori can be noted. Many of our towns, streets, lakes, rivers, mountains, trees and birds have Maori names and so accustomed have we become to many of them that we scarcely realise they are Maori. Linguistic experts could also provide many examples of how the Maori has influenced the everyday language of New Zealanders. One wonders, too, to what extent patterns of daily behaviour and social life, and even our institutions, have been modified through 150 years of association and through intermarriage. It would be strange indeed if Maori attitudes of thought, of living, of work and of play had not deeply affected our own thoughts, attitudes and ways of living.

What is being emphasised here is that while we are studying education's impact on the multi-racial society it must not be overlooked that the opposite also holds true.

Minorities other than the Maoris

Before proceeding to look more closely at Maori education, it seems wise to examine what educational arrangements have been made for other minority groups in New Zealand.

The immigration of foreign-speaking peoples to New Zealand has never been on as vast a scale as it has in such other countries as Canada or Australia. In Canada between 1948 and 1953 there were over 800,000 immigrants and 67 percent of these were from non-British countries, while in Australia, from 1945 to 1954, nearly 900,000 people arrived of whom some 460,000 or 51 percent came from countries where the mother tongue was other than English.[1]

In New Zealand, therefore, it has seldom been considered necessary to make special separate educational provisions for groups of immigrants. In the main, the new arrivals have scattered throughout the country and, except for Pahiatua where educational facilities were established for Polish immigrants and later served as a reception and training centre for 'displaced persons' and for one or two isolated small groups, no separate provisions have been made.

These remarks apply especially to children. For adults it has been possible to set up classes for instruction in the English language if six or more were available. There were many of these classes established after 1949 and nearly all of them appear to have followed a similar pattern: enthusiasm in the initial stages, and then a gradual falling away in attendance until finally the classes fell below the required number and they were discontinued. The reasons for this were many: once the immigrants acquired sufficient English to enable them to get along they no longer felt the need to attend, newly-acquired interests in other directions fully occupying their time, while many took up work elsewhere or moved to a different part of the country. One might also conclude either that the instruction was insufficiently interesting or effective or, alternatively that the teaching was so effective that the members of the class quickly gained an adequate mastery of the language.

There were many amusing stories told of these classes. For instance, at Titahi Bay where the impact of 140 male Austrians in their twenties and thirties caused some concern among the local bachelors, on one occasion a young man rather obviously consulted a small piece of cardboard and then approached a girl, stood at attention and said slowly: 'May-I-plees-dance-wis-you-plees?' The girl acquiesced and they danced in silence. Later consultation of the card brought a halting request to accompany the girl to her

---

[1] *Educational Studies and Documents*, 1955, vol. XVI, pp. 6, 7, 21.

home. On the way the girl said slowly: 'How-long-have-you-been-in-New-Zealand?'

'Huh! oh, been here all my life—but this is the only way to get a girl out nowadays.'

On another occasion the word 'desert' cropped up and the teacher explained carefully that it was a place where nothing grew. He then went on to deal with the word as a verb and tried to explain the meaning of 'A man might desert his wife'. A Dutchman piped up, 'You mean the words sound different, look the same, mean different? How would you say the man desert his wife because she is a place where nothing will grow?'

It is interesting to note that these classes were formed in widely separated places throughout the country, often near work-camps or large factories. For example, in 1945 there were over 100 classes, including those at Benhar, Otago, for Dutch, Germans, Hungarians and Swiss; at Roxburgh Hydro Works mainly for Dutch; at Dunedin for Austrians; at Golden Downs, Nelson, for mixed nationalities; at Balmoral State Forest for Polish and Dutch; at Titahi Bay for Austrians; at Cambridge for Dutch; at Levin and Wellington for Chinese; and at Gisborne and Rotorua for mixed groups.

The education of children

Because of the limitations of space we must be mainly concerned here with school age groups. The overall picture appears to have been that the children of new settlers attended the normal daily schools and carried out the normal type of programme. This practice seems consistent with New Zealand's educational philosophy—of equal opportunity for all, irrespective of race, creed or social status.

It is known that various national groups settled in different parts of the country, such as Dalmatians in North Auckland; Danes and Norwegians in the Manawatu, Norsewood and Dannevirke areas; the Syrians and Lebanese around the cities; but one can find little in the records to indicate that any special educational provision was made for them. It is true that some groups like the Italians and Greeks in Wellington have endeavoured to keep their own community and institutions and have, no doubt, taken steps to pass on to their children those ideas and customs of their own which they wish to be retained.

It can be assumed that because of their language problems, many immigrant pupils received extra attention and coaching from conscientious and sympathetic teachers and that in some cases parents arranged for extra tuition. From my own experience as a teacher and an inspector I know this to be the case.

All evidence points to the fact that the majority of these immigrants fitted easily into New Zealand schools and experienced little difficulty in their relationship with New Zealand children.

The Polish children's camp at Pahiatua

As has been mentioned, this camp was exceptional in that special provisions were made for education. Polish children arrived in November 1944 and the camp continued until the end of 1948. Primary and secondary schools were organised as Polish schools, taught by Polish teachers teaching from the official Polish syllabuses. The schools commenced with a total of 733 pupils—24 infants, 295 boys and 347 girls at the primary level, and 67 secondary pupils. Two New Zealand teachers were later appointed, to give instruction in English and about New Zealand customs; later, additional teachers were appointed to teach mathematics, science, physical education, and trades and sewing.

As the children proceeded to New Zealand schools and to employment, there was a steady fall in the roll numbers. At the beginning of 1946 they had fallen to 589, by 1947 to 387 and in 1948 to 251.

When it was decided to close the camp at the end of 1948, some changes were made in the organisation of the school. The Standard VI pupils continued to carry out the syllabus for the Polish Primary School Certificate, together with seven periods a week in English. The remainder of the school was organised on New Zealand lines and the New Zealand syllabus of instruction was used.

In his final report, the headmaster stated that the pupils who had proceeded to New Zealand schools found the first year difficult but once they became accustomed to the conditions there they competed on equal terms, and reports of their work had been very satisfactory.

From Pahiatua the pupils entered New Zealand schools, mostly Roman Catholic secondary schools.

Reception and training centre for displaced persons

When the Polish school closed down the Pahiatua camp was used as a reception and training centre for displaced persons who stayed there for a period of approximately three months. The first of three drafts of 926 persons, consisting of Latvians, Lithuanians, Estonians, Czechs, Poles, Russians, Ukrainians, Yugo-slavs, Rumanians and Croats, arrived at Pahiatua in June 1950 and of these 104 were of school age.

This first group was followed by two similar sized groups but with fewer pupils of school age. The main emphasis was on English, plus instruction in New Zealand's way of life—its customs and organisation. As more parents were placed in employment in different areas, the children entered local schools.

The present position

The steady flow of immigrants to New Zealand and the migration of large numbers of Maoris to urban centres have created new and serious problems for administrators, especially for educators, and none of these problems have a quick or easy solution.

The changes in rural areas are, in the main, more clear-cut and straightforward but the situation in urban areas is far more complex. A recent survey in the Auckland Education Board's district shows the proportion of non-European pupils in the schools. The survey, which excludes pupils of the Maori schools, gives a total of 18,563 non-Europeans representing 18 percent of the total rolls. Fifty-six of the 323 schools have 100 or more of such children, in 24 they constitute over 50 percent of the pupils and in 25 of the large schools they constitute more than one-third. Their backgrounds, levels of attainment, and the quality of English in these schools vary extensively. Perhaps the best way of appreciating the situation is to study the composition of three of the schools:

School A		School B		School C	
Maori	45	Maori	50	Maori	128
Samoan	25	Samoan	44	Samoan	15
Cook Is.	20	Cook Is.	66	Cook Is.	26
Niuean	21	Niuean	56	Niuean	3
Tongan	1	Tongan	1	Tongan	7
Indian	15	Indian	13	Fijian	1
Chinese	11	Chinese	13	Chinese	3
Others	5	Others	15	Others	4
	143		258		187

Total roll: 370.
Percentage of
non-European: 38.6.

Total roll: 307.
Percentage of
non-European: 84.

Total roll: 538
Percentage of
non-European: 35.

To assist schools with these very mixed groups and allow greater individual attention, additional teachers have been appointed, additional grants have been made for library material and teaching equipment, and a very pleasing feature has been the tangible support given by various business and welfare organisations.

In the schools, emphasis is placed on activity methods and on adjusting the work to the varying abilities of the pupils. As one headmaster expressed it: we endeavour to stress the importance of self-image through organising the programmes so that the child develops the self esteem and satisfaction that comes from a sense of achievement.

Besides teaching, these schools have to contend with many problems associated with the home and community. High rents often oblige both parents to work during the day and their children are left without proper supervision. To meet this situation many after-school activities have been organised by the school with the cooperation of various community agencies. One of the principal aims is to bring about a greater interest among parents in the work of the school. Homework classes, Brownie groups, music and basketball and other sports illustrate the type of activity being arranged.

While one can admire and appreciate what competent and understanding teachers are doing, these approaches highlight the difficulties of the changing situation and emphasise the urgency of all that has to be done, not only by the educational authorities but by all sections of the community, for these are indeed community problems which can be properly solved only by all interests working together.

Maori education

It is now time to examine the education of our largest non-European group—the Maori. The present situation cannot be clearly appreciated without some knowledge of their educational history.

The first known schools in New Zealand were established by the Anglican, Roman Catholic and Wesleyan missionaries for the education of Maoris. The chief objective of these schools was to convert the Maoris to Christianity as quickly as possible. The first teaching was mainly of a religious nature with reading and writing in the Maori language being taught through the Bible and Prayer Book. In addition, some practical crafts were taught, such as needlework for the girls and carpentry and agriculture for the boys.

In the early years, the New Zealand Government was content to leave the education of the Maori to the missionaries, but in 1858 assistance through subsidies and land grants was given on the condition that the language of instruction would be English. When the Native Schools Act was passed in 1867 provision was made for the establishment of Maori village schools which would be subject to Government inspection and which would be controlled by the Native Affairs Department. Except for the stipulation that all instruction was to be given in English, teachers were left free to decide what was to be taught.

Twelve years later the Education Department was created and the administration of native schools was transferred to it. A native schools' code or syllabus was compiled, and the Maori scholarship system was commenced, which has continued until the present time. One or two special provisions were made in staffing. Junior assistants were appointed as untrained teachers. They served as a link between Maori and pakeha; they helped the infant mistresses and other junior class teachers with the large numbers that prevailed in the lower part of the school, and they also helped to foster Maori culture. From 1940 onwards, the best of these junior assistants were able to enter a teachers' college and be trained as fully qualified teachers, but since 1948 the main recruitment of Maori teachers has come from pupils attending the various secondary schools.

Another special staffing provision was the appointment of married couples in the hope that such a combination would be able to play a wider and more significant part in community affairs. There is no doubt that in the early years these couples earned a high place in the esteem of the Maori people through the manner in which they devoted themselves to the health and welfare of Maori families in their districts. In recent times, much of the work that they were doing has been taken over by other agencies such as the Maori Welfare Officers, school nurses and visiting teachers, and the desirability of continuing the system of dual appointments has been questioned. However, while it proves difficult to secure the services of single teachers in isolated districts, the system will most likely be retained.

Racial decline

As Mr Mardle pointed out in a previous chapter, the impact of Western civilisation brought about a period of serious decline among the Maoris which lasted for some 50 years. The numbers fell to such a low level that it was feared that the Maori race might disappear completely. This decline caused administrators to look afresh at the needs of the Maori and, in 1930, a new education policy was enunciated, which stressed the importance of fostering selected Maori cultural aspects in the schools with the object of reviving in the Maoris a pride in themselves and in the past achievements of their race. This policy stressed the teaching of the English language as a necessary means of communication, the development of active as distinct from passive educational methods, the importance of desirable health habits, the teaching of Maori history, the teaching of selected Maori crafts, the teaching of simple housecraft to the girls and handicraft to the boys, and the fostering of rhythmic and aesthetic abilities.

Regret has sometimes been expressed that the teaching of the Maori language was not also included in the programme, and the issue has been raised many times since. While opinions have differed in the light of subsequent events, there seems a fair measure of agreement that Maori should not have been prohibited in those early years of settlement. Nevertheless, it should be noted that it was not only the pakehas who insisted on English being the only language of instruction, but that there were leading Maoris who were themselves firmly of this opinion. As the years have passed and more and more Maori children come to school knowing little or nothing of the Maori language, there is only an occasional request for the teaching of Maori at the primary school. The difficulties of introducing the subject have also increased. Even in the few areas where the children come to school speaking Maori, a suitable teacher of the language has to be found and there could be no guarantee how long he would stay in the district. The agreement of the parents is also required. At Ruatoki, for example, an area where the children spoke Maori, a play-centre or kindergarten was planned and the Department of Education suggested that as a Maori-speaking teacher was available Maori might be the language of the centre. The parents, however, strongly opposed the idea on the grounds that they wanted their youngsters to learn English at the earliest possible moment.

The first half of the twentieth century

From 1900 there was at first a steady, but from 1936 onwards a rapid increase in Maori population. With this growth came a marked change in the attitudes and outlook of the Maori people, aptly described in a previous chapter as 'a reanimation of the spirit'. The new educational measures introduced into the schools in 1930 also had their effect and were followed by a period of noticeable progress. As a result, over the years the Maori people have developed a genuine pride in the work and achievements of their schools, and, while attitudes are changing, they look warily at any suggested changes of control.

The National Committee on Maori Education

As the Maori school population increased, requiring new schools to be built often within range of existing public schools, as families moved to another part of the country, as the social and economic conditions of the Maoris changed, as more and more organisations began to take an active interest in Maori education, it became increasingly apparent that the whole administration of Maori education needed re-examination and, in 1955, the Government called together a National Committee on which there was strong Maori representation, to survey the whole problem and to bring down recommendations. Since that time the National Committee has met annually and has served as an excellent link between the organisations and communities they represent, and the educational authorities.

Among the original Committee's 29 resolutions and recommendations, the most far-reaching were that:

(1) New Zealand should work towards a uniform system of education for Maori and pakeha.

(2) Maori school committees should be given the full responsibilities enjoyed by board school committees.

(3) Greater emphasis should be placed on Maori culture in all schools, board as well as Maori.

(4) An officer for Maori education should be appointed for the purpose of bringing about closer coordination among the various organisations concerned with Maori education.

Progress has been made in all of these directions. I shall refer to them in reverse order. The fourth Officer for Maori Education has recently been appointed; Maori history, arts and crafts are included in most school programmes; and Maori school committees are functioning well and taking a pride in their new responsibilities. The policy of transfer of Maori schools to board control has been proceeded with, but care is always taken that transfer takes place only after consultation and with the agreement of the parents of the school concerned. Twenty-two schools have transferred since 1955 and about the same number have closed through consolidation with neighbouring schools. The recent Commission on Education supported the policy and suggested that the transfer might be completed in about 10 years.

Although in areas where there were native schools attendance was compulsory from 1884, few Maori pupils attended public schools until regulations in 1903 compelled them to enrol at public schools if there was no native school in the locality.

Expansion of European settlement, movement of Maori population and compulsory attendance resulted in a sharp rise in the number of Maori children attending board schools, and since about 1910 the number in these schools has exceeded the number in Maori schools. The growth has been exceedingly rapid, from approximately 12,000 in 1910 to just under 46,000 in 1965. These pupils are spread throughout some 1,600 public primary schools.

On the other hand, the tendency has been for the rolls in Maori schools to decrease until in July 1965 there were 8,754 or only 18 percent of Maori children in Maori schools. In addition, there were 2,898 Maori children attending private primary schools.

The situation today

In a survey of this length it would be impossible to give a clear and complete picture of Maori education. The situation varies so greatly from district to district, from community to community, from school to school and even from classroom to classroom that it is almost impossible to generalise without qualification. As John Watson has pointed out in his *Horizons of Unknown Power,* this is true of all aspects of Maori life.

I shall restrict myself therefore to some of the most important features and problems of Maori education. I should like to have described to you in detail a typical Maori primary school classroom, but will content myself by saying that it is usually a place where there is a pleasant, homely atmosphere, where happy relationships exist between teacher and taught, where regular periods are conducted in oral and written English, spelling, reading, arithmetic, social studies (with Maori history and customs occupying a prominent place), music, arts and crafts, and physical education. Methods will vary from teacher to teacher but, in the main, they will be based on past experience and the latest findings of research. If we take reading as an example, the techniques employed will most likely be a combination of look-and-say, sentence, pictorial clues, phonic and structural analysis, and the reading material will be closely related to the vocabularies and interests of young children.

For historical, cultural, social and economic reasons, many of which are well known, standards of achievement vary considerably. It is therefore not easy to visualise how anything but limited success could result from 'crash programmes' that are so freely advocated at the present time. New Zealanders as a whole have accepted the principle of educating for individual differences, but many do not understand what this means in actual classroom practice. What type of crash programme, in what subject, could prove successful in dealing with pupils with such widely differing backgrounds and in such differing social and geographical situations, and with such varying abilities and temperaments?

English and reading

The two subjects of the curriculum in which standards of achievement are subject to the most criticism are English and reading. In general, it is true that when Maori pupils enter secondary schools their mastery of the English language is not as good as that of their pakeha schoolmates and this comparative weakness is reflected in their progress in almost every other subject. But can any crash programme bring about any quick or comprehensive improvement?

For some 125 years now, thousands of able, conscientious teachers using the best known methods have concentrated on improving their Maori pupils' mastery of English. They have been assisted by school inspectors, by organising teachers, by research, by means of bulletins, magazine articles and through extensive in-service training courses. Sometimes the stress has been on grammar but mostly it has been on oral and written English.

Within recent years especially, great importance has been attached to oral discussion and written assignments based on topics that have had significant interest for the pupils. While there is much that could be criticised about both past and present methods of teaching English, the overall picture is one of efficient teaching. The teaching of English has been made so much more difficult owing to the wide variation in the quality of English of Maori pupils at entry. Well into this century, a majority of pupils came to school from homes where only Maori was spoken. As time went on the position became more complicated, until now most children come to school with English as their chief means of communication even if there is a wide range in its quality and though it is, in some cases, a mixture of poor English, slang and Maori. The number of young Maoris who have grown up using only the English language is steadily increasing. Research workers, too, are providing educators with fresh knowledge and insight into the language difficulties of Maori children, and schools are testing out many of their recommendations. Within recent years, valuable contributions have been made in language studies by I. H. Barham, L. Anderson, A. Aitken and by R. A. Benton.

Many of the comments already made about the teaching of English also hold true of reading. Excellent results have been achieved by some teachers in both rural and urban areas, but the results are, again, subject to wide variation. They are limited, too, by the child's concepts which, in turn, are the result of his past experiences.

It is possible, through modern techniques, to develop a high degree of mechanical accuracy and fluency in reading, but unless these are constantly related to the child's understanding these skills are of little value. Concepts are based on experience and are unlikely to be acquired through any crash programme.

Cities like Chicago in America, realising the need to widen the experience of thousands of handicapped Negro and other children in their areas, have arranged special summer vacation courses for them. A large portion of the time of these courses is devoted to visits to zoos, institutions, factories, business concerns, railway yards, shipyards, airports and the like. These visits are followed by discussions and lessons on what has been seen. Reports and records of these projects indicate a noticeable difference in the work of the pupils on their return to their normal schools.

In line with overseas countries, New Zealand is becoming increasingly aware of the significance of the pre-school years in establishing a sound basis for future learning, and the pre-school services are rapidly expanding. The Maori Education Foundation and the Maori Affairs Department must be given credit for providing stimulus and assistance in this field.

I have spent some time on these features of our schools because I do not believe that many problems connected with Maori education can be solved through any sudden revolution in teaching practices.

In fairness to many of those who advocate crash programmes, it has to be pointed out that most are concerned to see a substantial increase in finance and in staffing. It cannot be denied that additional money could be used to advantage in many ways, nor can it be denied that an increase in staffing would prove of great benefit, especially if this increase improved the teacher-pupil ratio in the first two years of school life, for it is in this period that attitudes of success or failure can be induced. But again I stress that while these extra provisions will help, they cannot overcome quickly the various handicaps suffered by Maori children for cultural, social, economic or any other reason.

The transition from primary to secondary school often proves an unsettling and difficult process for many Maori children. Some of them have already attended at least four primary schools and have experienced frequent changes of teachers. Each change means a new adjustment, and if the child is already inclined to be shy or self-conscious and is well aware of his backwardness, his sense of inadequacy increases. Added to this, he has far too often found himself classified in the lowest forms at his new high school.

In fairness to secondary schools, it must be stated that many of these now face a decidedly different situation from what they were accustomed to. Instead of one or two Maori pupils entering their schools as they have in the past, now large numbers enter, bringing with them different needs and different problems. New Zealand has, in fact, reached the stage where 99 percent of Maori pupils proceed to secondary school.

The secondary schools are meeting the new challenges in many ways, and some have modified their classification to avoid any suggestion that the Maoris are in any way inferior pupils. Some schools have organised tutorial and remedial reading classes, and others have arranged for the supervision of homework. For some years now, an enthusiastic committee of the New Zealand Post-Primary Teachers' Association has been functioning with its sole objective the improvement of education for Maori pupils.

Before I conclude this section on the work of the schools I must mention briefly some of the other steps being taken to improve the education of Maori people.

Since the State took over the control of Maori schools, scholarships have been granted to enable promising pupils to attend secondary boarding schools. These scholarships (about 100 each year) are available to Maori children in both Maori and board schools. Six or more university scholarships are also available to pupils who have succeeded at secondary schools. The Maori Education Foundation also provides generous assistance to promising pupils and in 1965 distributed over 1,000 grants valued at £78,000.

I have already referred to special staffing provisions made for Maori schools. In addition, school inspectors keep an idea of standards, interpret new syllabuses, pass on new ideas and arrange in-service training courses; organising teachers, reading and infant advisers, and art, music, physical education and nature study specialists also make valuable contributions. Extra finance is also made available for the purchase of library books and teaching material where there is a proven need.

Besides these regular provisions, valuable assistance is given by such agencies as the Department of Maori Affairs and the Maori Education Foundation. It would be impossible here to acknowledge the many ways in which these bodies assist. Suffice it to say that an Inter-Departmental Committee of Maori Affairs and Education meets regularly to discuss problems connected with Maori education.

No mention has so far been made of the work of the Officer for Maori Education, but he occupies a key role in formulating policy, in fostering Maori education and in coordinating the work of the numerous organisations concerned with it.

Education of the public

It is obvious from many comments on Maori education that far too many people are uninformed and quite unaware of the true situation. How to overcome this and provide up-to-date information is not easy to see. It is extremely difficult to give a full and correct account of what is happening at any particular point of time. The situation varies so much and one is inclined to make generalisations about a most complex situation.

Many different institutions and organisations are concerned with Maori education. To mention some of these: pre-school, primary, secondary and university teachers; school committees and governing boards; the Maori Affairs, Health, Labour, Housing, Child Welfare and Education Departments; Maori tribal committees and the Maori Women's Welfare Leagues; the National Committee on Maori Education and the Education Board Maori Committees; the New Zealand Educational Institute and its branches; the Post-Primary Teachers' Association; the Maori Education Foundation; the Parents-Teachers' Association and the various Education Progressive Associations. Each of these groups assists in keeping public opinion informed, especially about its own activities. The press also plays its part and, within recent years, there have been many fine articles by leading newspapers. The production of at least two excellent films has stimulated interest and enlightened the public on aspects of Maori life about which they were unfamiliar. Further films, concentrating on schools and educational institutions, would assist in conveying the true story. I should also like to see the television service from time to time showing actual Maori and mixed racial groups of children at work in the classroom.

I do not underestimate the value of informed criticism in bringing about improvements, but I should like to see more newspapers and magazines devote space to factual and interesting articles on Maori education, especially those that feature Maori successes.

The future

It seems inevitable, with so much attention focused on the education of Maori and other racial groups, that there will be pressure for additional finance, increased staffing, more specialists, further testing and research, and for more effective teaching in English and reading. These are all pleasing indications of the growing interest and concern of the dominant society for the less fortunate sections, but it must be repeated that there are limits to what can and should be done. No matter what changes are advocated, their success in the end depends upon what actually happens in the classroom or, expressed in another way, the success of any scheme depends upon many different teachers in many different situations, teaching children with many different needs.

Despite these words of warning I believe there are many reasons for being optimistic about the future.

There have been noticeable changes in the attitude of Maori parents towards further education. This is evidenced by the 200 adults who enrolled in School Certificate classes last year; more and more are realising that entry to the professions, commerce and more skilled occupations is dependent upon educational qualifications; the number of young Maori parents who have attended secondary school is steadily increasing. Research overseas is pointing to better ways of tackling problems connected with multi-racial societies; and the new linguistic approaches to the teaching of English look most promising. The wider use of teaching machines, tape recorders and projectors will also have an effect and I hope that the time is not too far distant when the use of educational television will be extended in our schools. Already, rural and urban teachers report that they receive the best response in oral and written English when their teaching is related to television sessions.

There are still many important problems to be overcome. Although a wide range of courses is available in our secondary schools, because of the exaggerated importance placed on School Certificate (and for other reasons) secondary courses are not always as realistic as they might be for children obviously not proceeding to university. Changes in the School Certificate examination are at present under consideration and when they are implemented I am hopeful that they will provide fresh and more realistic incentives for the less academic children. Too often the results of education are judged solely on an academic basis. Numerous examples could be quoted of people who were considered far from bright at school but who later have proved outstanding in their own fields of endeavour.

I referred earlier to the Maori's natural attraction to the concrete and immediate rather than to the abstract and remote. Some Maoris have proved successful at universities, in the professions and in other positions of responsibility, but should we expect, at this stage of their history, as high a proportion of passes among Maoris as their contemporaries in School Certificate, University Entrance and degree examinations? New Zealanders certainly have a duty to encourage Maoris and members of other racial groups to continue with their education, and I have no doubt that with the encouragement now being given in many ways, the numbers who go on to higher institutions will steadily increase, but it may be years before they will reach pakeha proportions.

I agree with the recommendation of the Commission of Enquiry into Vocational Training that children should be given a good education before specialisation, and that specialisation should not begin too early, but the fact remains that many of our less academic pupils leave soon after they reach the age of 15 because our schools are unable to offer incentives attractive enough to compete with those outside. During my visit to the United States I was impressed with the way in which what they describe as 'Co-operative Education' was working. In this scheme, children worked at school in the morning and then gained experience in various occupations in the afternoons. It was claimed that the school, the employers and the children benefited and that those children who took part in the scheme tended to stay longer at school because they could see the value of continuing their studies. I believe that similar schemes could prove successful in some parts of New Zealand.

In summing up, I wish to emphasise two points.

First, many of the educational problems of our multi-racial society cannot be solved by teachers and educators alone but only by all sections of the community working together. Backwardness or delinquency may be caused through unsatisfactory housing conditions, through poor health, through a lack of out-of-school provision for recreation and hobbies, or even because of the attitudes of neighbours and the community giving rise to reactions of bewilderment, anxiety, retreat or resistance.

Second, there is a grave danger that continuous criticism and judgments by pakehas on Maori behaviour and on their comparative failures in school examinations, will have the opposite effect to what is desired. From my discussions with many Maori people, I have gained the impression that they are becoming sensitive and, in some cases, even resentful at continually have their deficiencies made public.

I believe that what is needed at the present time is a boosting of Maori morale through a recognition of their achievements in many fields and of the many valuable contributions they have made to New Zealand's way of life. Perhaps many of the Maori people would settle for less than this, preferring far less spotlight and instead to be regarded as ordinary New Zealanders whose special needs will be treated on the same basis as the special needs of any other group.

Urbanisation and
the Multi-racial Society

J. M. McEWEN

In the course of my duties I have had contact with five Polynesian minorities in New Zealand: Maori, Samoan, Cook Islands Maori, Niuean and Tokelauan. The movement of these various groups to New Zealand cities is very similar in many respects and different in others.

The reasons for migration are much the same, although not necessarily the same in relative importance: they are both economic and social.

Economic reasons for migration

There is no doubt that the lack of regular employment in the isolated country districts and the consequent low and irregular income is one of the principal reasons for the movement of rural Maoris to the cities. This is also true for the island communities. As new incentives have arisen the country Maori and the islander have felt the need for greater earnings. One of the principal incentives is a modern standard of housing. The unpainted shack or the thatched *fale* have ceased to be adequate but their replacement costs a great deal of money. Before the establishment of the Government housing loan scheme in the Cooks, it was very common for a man to migrate to Auckland to obtain work until such time as he had saved the cost of materials for a new house.

Many men then returned home and built a house, but many others decided to settle in New Zealand and sent for their wives and families.

Both here and in the islands the rapid increase of the Polynesian people has caused economic stresses that have forced people to migrate to an urban centre. The inadequacy of family land to support the more numerous families has been a prime factor in the Maori movement to the cities. The same applies to Rarotonga, parts of Western Samoa and to the Tokelau Islands. Niue, on the other hand, is underpopulated and land shortage is not generally a cause for emigration.

So far as the Maoris are concerned, there has been widespread discontent with low incomes and poor living standards. It is not generally realised that the deplorable state of Maori housing for the first 40 or 50 years of this century was due to the fact that it was impossible for the average Maori to finance a new home. No lending institution in the country would advance money on the security of Maori land with many owners, and very few Maoris had the remotest chance of finding capital once the wholesale alienation of land ceased in the early years of the century. It was not until the passing of the Maori Housing Act 1935 that capital could be obtained. Once money is borrowed a regular income becomes a necessity.

Social reasons for migration

What are usually called 'the bright lights' are undoubtedly of importance in urbanisation. Those who are not acquainted with the unutterable boredom of village life on a tiny island could never appreciate how strongly people yearn for the exciting life they hear of from their relatives in New Zealand cities. Particularly does this apply to atolls, where the people probably live a more circumscribed life than any other people in the world, including the Eskimos. Films and radio have penetrated to the waybacks of New Zealand and to the Pacific Islands. What has been a satisfying life for centuries has suddenly become unacceptably dull and the cities have become a sort of composite Paradise and Eldorado.

The lack of educational opportunity for children has also played its part. Despite the tremendous improvement in education during the past few years in the isolated Maori districts and in the islands, the curricula are limited of necessity and the competition is less keen. Many Maori and island parents have moved to the cities to give their children the benefits of the better education in city schools.

Another important factor is the movement of families to rejoin children or other relatives who have settled in the towns. It is a common practice for islanders to save up the price of ship or air fares to bring their parents or their brothers and sisters to New Zealand.

Finally, there is the high sense of adventure which Polynesian people have not yet lost. They have always wanted to know what was over the horizon and they still want to know. The limitations of small isolated communities may have a lot to do with this.

Extent of urbanisation

In 1926 only 8.7 percent of the Maori population lived in cities and boroughs. By 1951 this figure had risen to 18.7 percent. At this point the movement gained impetus and at the 1961 census 33.3 percent of Maoris lived in urban areas. A Maori Affairs Department estimate is that by 1970 over 56 percent of Maoris will live in these areas, a total of over 132,000 people. The rural Maori population is expected to be almost stationary during the next few years while the urban population expands at a very high rate.

At the time of the 1961 census the island population of New Zealand was as follows:

Samoan	6,481
Cook Islanders	4,499
Niuean	1,728
Other Polynesian	1,632
	14,340

About half of this number lived in Auckland. The distribution of the island groups varies. Samoans have settled mainly in Auckland, Wellington and Christchurch; Niueans in Auckland and Wellington; while Cook Island Maoris have spread throughout the country with sizeable communities in Auckland, Tokoroa, Hawke's Bay, Wellington and Southland. The Tokelauans are concentrated mainly in Wellington. In all cases the settlements have grown round nuclei formed by a few original settlers. An interesting fact revealed by the 1961 census was that almost 40 percent of the island Polynesians were born in New Zealand. At a rough estimate the island community would now be about 19,000 or 20,000.

Problems arising from urbanisation

The movement of rural or island people to the cities brings about a number of problems, both social and economic. Principal amongst the economic problems are housing and other accommodation, the management of finance, and to a lesser extent, employment.

Housing

Until the introduction of the capitalisation of family benefit, the immigrants into cities had grave problems in obtaining houses. Since then the situation has become easier, but in view of the low average income of Polynesian people and the larger families, it is still a problem. Not many years ago the greater number of houses built by the Maori Affairs Department were in rural areas. The change in the situation even in the last few years is quite spectacular. In 1961, 55 percent of the houses were built in urban areas, Auckland and Wellington accounting for 25.7 percent. In 1965 the proportion built in the cities was 75.2 percent, Auckland and Wellington amounting to 35.2 percent.

The greatest difficulty in the main centres is that of obtaining building sites within the price range that Maori families can afford. Almost inevitably Maori homes are being built increasingly in the more distant and less attractive suburbs. The best cure for this is of course to ensure that more and more Maoris are trained for the higher paid skilled trades and professions.

The Maori housing scheme is not the only source of building finance available to Maoris; it is in fact an additional source, and many Maoris finance homes through the State Advances Corporation and other institutions. Until recently the serious state of Maori housing generally was partially dealt with by way of a special allocation of State rental homes in certain localities. With the improvement which has taken place in recent years this is no longer the practice, but many Maori families are still obtaining State rental houses in the usual way.

At the request of the Minister of Island Territories, the housing of islanders in Auckland was surveyed in 1965 by the School of Social Science of Victoria University. The survey showed that the islanders were generally managing extraordinarily well to house themselves without any initial capital resources. However, it was apparent that the time was near when some special assistance may be necessary. The most undesirable feature of island settlement in Auckland is the concentration of so many people in the centre of the city in the same areas which had a concentration of Maori families 15 or 20 years ago. With housing assistance the Maoris have largely moved out to the suburbs and the problems they faced some years ago are now confronting the islanders.

Accommodation for single people

It cannot be denied that the Maori girl or boy who moves to the city to work or to study has even more difficulty than a pakeha in obtaining a reasonable place in which to live. This has led over the years to the establishment of hostels and blocks of flats. Including buildings now in progress, the Maori Affairs Department and the Maori Trustee have provided or subsidised accommodation in Auckland, Wellington and Christchurch to the extent of 11 hostels for 430 boys and eight hostels for 295 girls. In addition, blocks of flats have been built or purchased to cater for another 65 girls. Further accommodation for single Maoris is projected.

Apart from the facilities mentioned, accommodation is also provided by various church organisations and by the Labour Department.

The management of finance

The Maori who has moved from a remote country district to the city is faced with financial problems far greater than he has met before. The idea of budgeting his income is a foreign one. He is faced with rent or mortgage instalments, high rates, insurance, travelling expenses, more costly clothing, more opportunities for entertainment, more alluring arrays of goods in the shops and above all, the slick salesman who is not over-worried as to whether hire-purchase instalments are within his reach or not. Almost inevitably a large proportion of the Maori immigrants to the cities are deeply into debt in a short time. The seriousness of this situation led, a few years ago, to the establishment of a voluntary budgetary advisory service. In many parts of New Zealand, public-spirited citizens are spending much of their spare time advising Maori families how to plan their expenditure and remove their burdens of debt. The Maori Affairs Department is sponsoring this scheme and a steady expansion is taking place. It is interesting that a growing proportion of European families is being helped, also.

The ideal time, of course, to educate people in such matters is before they are faced with new difficulties. The problem here, however, is that the great majority of immigrants to the cities move independently because they reach a decision to do so, not because of any planned resettlement scheme. Recently, however, an experimental approach has been made to the problem. The pre-employment course for 60 young Maoris who came to Wellington together in January 1966 included instruction at the Wellington Polytechnic in simple economics and money matters.

The island people who migrate independently to the cities seem to manage somewhat better than the rural Maori. I think this may be because of the realisation that they have burned their boats and have to stand on their own feet. They lack the escape route back to the village if things go wrong.

In the resettlement of some of the Tokelau Islanders in New Zealand, it is planned to provide instruction in the management of finance. This is most necessary as the Tokelauans have little money and little use for money in their atoll economy.

Employment

Generally speaking, Maori and other Polynesian migrants to the cities have no difficulty in obtaining employment. The principal problem is the type of employment. Because of a relatively low standard of educational attainment, the only class of work available to most of the migrants is unskilled labour. All too often, also, a young Maori who has better qualifications will accept highly paid casual labour because of the immediate monetary gain. Maori Welfare Officers and Vocational Guidance Officers are paying increasing attention to the steering of young people into work which offers better long-term prospects. The pre-employment course for young Maoris already referred to resulted in the placement of a number of youths and girls in very much better types of work than they would have otherwise obtained.

One of the more spectacular remedies for the lack of skilled Maori tradesmen is the Maori Affairs trade-training scheme which started some years ago and which has been considerably extended in the last few years. This scheme is centred round the Institutes of Technology in Auckland, Wellington and Christchurch. At present, 144 Maori lads are enrolled each year for apprenticeships in carpentry, painting and paperhanging, plastering, plumbing, motor mechanics, panel beating, and electrical wiring. After an initial period of trade training and formal education (two years in the case of carpenters and less in other cases), the boys go to private employers to complete their terms of apprenticeship. This scheme is resulting in an output of hundreds of skilled Maori tradesmen, very few of whom would ever have qualified otherwise. That this is an advantage to the country as a whole as well as to the Maori lads concerned, few would deny.

But the basic problem remains—that of the generally low standard of education which prevents any significant proportion of Maoris or islanders from entering professions and highly skilled occupations. Progress is being made, however, and the work of the Maori Education Foundation and special measures being adopted by the Education Department are beginning to show results. As Maori and European are for the first time in general and continuous contact as a result of the Maori move to the cities, the importance of fitting Maoris for all types of trades and professions cannot be overstressed. The danger to our society of what Ernest Beaglehole called 'a brown-skinned proletariat' is an obvious one; apart from that our country cannot, in this technological age, afford the economic waste of having thousands of potentially skilled Maoris in unskilled occupations simply because they lack the necessary basic education.

Social problems

The influx of comparatively unsophisticated and comparatively ill-educated people into the cities gives rise to many problems. Young people who have lived in a more or less communal society are very apt to go astray in the highly individualistic life of the city. It is appreciated by far too few pakeha New Zealanders that although Maori society has undergone many changes in the last century and a half, it is still a different society from that of the suburban pakeha. The Maori coming to the city quickly realises this and is inclined to feel insecure in a strange environment which is unfriendly and indifferent to him. It is small wonder that the less inhibited atmosphere of the hotel bar becomes attractive. It is understandable, too, that the Maori youth is inclined to draw attention to himself by adopting the most extreme forms of hair style and clothing which immediately cause the staider pakeha to classify him with the irresponsible misfits in city society. Unfortunately, too, the irresponsible element welcomes him and the chance of drifting into crime becomes a real one. Statistics show that the Maori is not generally a calculating criminal—the crimes he commits are more often unsophisticated and impulsive. With maturity the Maori crime rate drops more steeply than that of the pakeha, but it is far too high in adolescence and early adulthood. As educational standards improve and more satisfying occupations become available, these factors together with a better adjustment to urban life should tend to reduce the crime rate as time goes on.

The crime record of the island immigrants is quite different. Statistics show that serious offences are comparatively rare. The principal troubles are those arising from liquor, such as assault. The great majority of islanders in New Zealand are law-abiding citizens and this is in no small measure due to the influence of the churches which are still the focal centre for most island communities. It is unfortunate that the publicity given to an occasional serious offence committed by an islander has given the public a totally false impression.

Apart from crime, the Maori and island migrants are apt to become unpopular with their pakeha neighbours because of their high-spirited way of enjoying themselves. Any group of Polynesians enjoying a social occasion will sooner or later burst into song and uninhibited laughter which is unacceptable in our suburban society. People who are used to open spaces and who have not yet lost the capacity to enjoy themselves do not readily adapt their ways to staid suburbia but I suppose they will in time become as mirthless and as tuneless as the rest of us. That Maoris also have drunken parties is true. That Europeans frequently do the same is equally true, but a Maori neighbour would be less inclined to complain about it. The Maori is more generous, too, in that he does not consider all pakehas to be noisy and drunken because one of his neighbours is so inclined.

A serious problem for the Maori coming to a city is the loneliness and the feeling of not belonging. In the area where I live there are a number of Maori families. I discovered a few years ago that the majority of the Maori housewives, even those married to Europeans, seldom went outside their front gates except to go shopping. They were living in the community without belonging to it. This was almost entirely due to a sense of diffidence in European company, not to any wish to live in seclusion. The situation has been cured by the formation of a lively Maori club in the district to which Europeans are welcome. The association with Europeans in the club has given the women confidence and their whole way of life has changed. I am satisfied that Maoris and Europeans get to know each other much more readily in a Maori atmosphere than in a European atmosphere. This is a sad commentary on our stiff and unfriendly society. The value of Maori youth clubs and other organisations in the cities is very great. The very good Maori-pakeha relations in Wellington are in no small measure due to the part played in civic life by Ngati Poneke, founded 30 years ago, and to other newer clubs.

One of the profoundest effects of the Maori movement to the cities from the point of view of our national future is its effect on intermarriage. Over the past few years the Maori Affairs Department has conducted a house-to-house survey of Maori living conditions throughout the North Island except greater Auckland, greater Wellington, and Hamilton. One of the items in the survey was the number of mixed marriages. The survey covered over 20,000 families, and the proportion of families where the husband or wife was a full European was almost 12 percent. In the cities, however, the proportion was much higher, ranging from 13 percent to as high as 35.3 percent in Palmerston North. In the days when the majority of Maoris lived in the remoter country districts, Maori and European lived on amicable terms but tended to go their own way. In the cities where young Maoris and Europeans work together, travel together and dance together, the chances of intermarriage increase enormously, and this is what is happening and will happen at an increasing rate.

What is going on in the Maori world today is a revolution—a revolution as tremendous and as far-reaching to the Maori as the Industrial Revolution was to society in England a couple of centuries ago. The English people did not get through it unscathed and nor will the Maori. That he gets through it with as little stress as possible is of the greatest importance not only to him but to every one of us if we have any interest in the sort of society our grandchildren will live in.

The policy of integration

The policy of the New Zealand Government in relation to Maori Affairs is one of integration. As Dr Metge has pointed out in her paper, this is a policy which guarantees the same rights and opportunities to all citizens whatever their group membership may be. To this guarantee of rights and opportunities we should add that equal responsibilities are also involved. To achieve integration, special measures are recognised as being necessary where an ethnic group is at present suffering under special handicaps or lack of opportunities. Such special measures in New Zealand include the Maori Education Foundation, Maori housing, the Maori apprenticeship scheme and so on. The object of these schemes is to remove what are at present barriers to integration.

Unfortunately the word 'integration' varies in meaning according to the views of the person using it, but the present Government policy interprets integration as a state of affairs where no citizen differs from any other citizen, because of his ethnic origin, in his economic and social rights, opportunities and responsibilities. On the other hand the policy of integration does not mean that an individual is not free to choose his own cultural pursuits; it does not mean that Maoris will be compelled to abandon their own historical or traditional background. There are those who decry Maori clubs in the cities as being exclusive organisations which encourage segregation and racialism. In fact the converse is true in that almost every Maori club welcomes non-Maori members. New Zealand is not harmed by the existence of Caledonian societies or Welsh clubs, nor will it be harmed by Maori clubs. Although many Europeans obviously treat 'integration' and 'assimilation' as synonyms, the Maori people generally prefer to think of integration as a policy which does not mean the disappearance of Maori institutions and everything that distinguishes a Maori from other people. In this I agree with them.

If full integration is achieved, it is my view that it will not stop there. The figures I have quoted on intermarriage show that what will happen in the long run will not be greatly affected by policies or theories. The fusion of our people by intermarriage at an increasing rate will inevitably result in social, economic and cultural fusion. What we must try to ensure is that the New Zealander of the future will be proud of his mixed origin and tradition and that he will not be simply a displaced Briton with a tendency towards brown eyes and black hair. As I see it, integration is a two-way process.

Welfare Requirements in a Multi-racial Society

L. G. ANDERSON

Introduction

Welfare services are social services. The terms are almost synonymous. During the last 20 years or so the volume of books and periodicals and other writings on social service and social work has grown enormously. Over more recent years there has been an increased output of writings about racialism and about the need for peoples of all races to live together in peace. Because of these two developments it would be a bold person who today would lay claim to have anything spectacularly new to say on the topic of multi-racial social work and welfare requirements. I am certainly not such a person. Accordingly the reader will look in vain for dramatic newsworthy solutions to the problem of providing the efficient welfare services peculiar to the needs of a multi-racial society. What I can do is to give a factual summary of what I believe to be the present position in New Zealand, to comment on it and to incorporate a few not very original ideas on where we should be heading.

Although I am describing the ideas I put forward as 'not very original', nevertheless they are based on my own practical experience. I am a third generation New Zealander. I have never been to Europe. Whenever I am required to answer a question on an official form about my race and am restricted in what I can answer,

I write 'European' but add that I object to such a classification. I am not, and never have been, a European; I am a New Zealander. I went to school happily with Maori and pakeha children without being aware during my childhood that I was in a multi-racial group. Some of our teachers, dedicated and well-meaning, talked what I now know was a lot of arrant nonsense about 'the yellow peril' which led me for years to presume incorrectly, not only that all Orientals were crafty and cunning and intent on over-running the rest of us, but also that Orientals were the coloured people. Negroes didn't qualify, except as sentimental characters in romantic stories and songs. It never entered my head to associate my Maori friends with coloured people or with people of a separate race from ours.

For most of my adult life I have been engaged in social work. Apart from a fairly wide range of activities in voluntary social work, my main jobs have been in the Child Welfare Division of the Department of Education, first as a field officer in three parts of New Zealand, two of which have a large Maori population providing a predominance of clients, and later as an administrator in Wellington. I am now in charge of what is, in fact, the largest welfare service in the country, employing over 1,000 persons full time. I have worked closely with Maori colleagues in social service departments in New Zealand. I am implacably opposed to all forms of racial discrimination. In order to suggest that I have earned the right to criticise my Maori friends when I think criticism is justified, I am choosing to mention that, after a lifelong interest in rugby football, after considerable experience as a rugby commentator on the radio and after developing a personal acquaintance with and respect for some of the prominent South African footballers, in 1965 I practised a personal boycott of the games played by the visiting South African rugby team in New Zealand because of its composition in accordance with the principles of apartheid. I waved no banners and joined no processions, but salved my own conscience in the way I though best and most logical. My boycott caused no financial loss to the various rugby unions, whose grounds were filled to capacity anyway. It influenced no one. It did, however, seem to be consistent with my representation of New Zealand at the United Nations Social Commission, with my cordial relationship with coloured people everywhere, with my status as a social worker and with my endeavours to be a practising Christian.

Development of the welfare state

I hope that from my comments will emerge a picture of what I consider the welfare requirements of a multi-racial state to be. I prefer this to a tabulated recipe setting out what requirements, theoretically, should be, as though one could serve a useful purpose in stating these in isolation, disregarding the materials we have to work with, the climate we are working in and the machinery already in operation. We cannot set out from a cold start. We can improve our practices, but not entirely abolish them and replace them with a completely new policy. Progress does not work that way. The whole history of the development of our welfare services in New Zealand has been one of practical measures undertaken to relieve immediate need in the manner that appeared appropriate at the time. The passage of time and the results of research can, and do, serve to show that much of what we did was lacking in professional skill and ineffective. This will always be so. Social work needs cannot wait for research to produce findings. We must always do the best we can in good faith with the tools we have and run the risk of learning later that we could have done better had we known more and had better tools. In social work one must learn by doing as well as by studying. Social work practices cannot be learned in a vacuum, nor can emergencies wait. In saying this, I would not like to create the impression that I underestimate the value of academic training for social workers.

The history of New Zealand has been one of fairly continuous development and expansion of social services. This, I believe, reflects credit on all our political leaders. As a taxpayer and a citizen (if I can ignore what my official job is), I am proud to be associated with a country which is enlightened enough to be openly a welfare state and to feel no need to apologise for it. One of the distinguishing marks of a truly civilised country is the willingness of its people, through their elected representatives, to accept responsibility for helping those who, because of infirmity, physical or mental handicaps, social inadequacy or any other disability, are unable to cope satisfactorily with life by their own efforts.

The principal welfare requirements, and hence services, in New Zealand are concerned with health, housing, social security, education (including pre-school services), child welfare, vocational guidance, marriage guidance, probation and legal aid for offenders.

As appendices to this paper, I attach statements kindly supplied by the Chairman of the Social Security Commission, the Secretary for Maori Affairs, and the Secretary for Justice. These statements, together with one about the work of the Child Welfare Division, will serve to give to those not familiar with our main social services, an outline of their functions. The Director-General of Health was also asked whether he would submit a similar statement for publication. With typical succinctness, Dr Kennedy replied that 'at the risk of being thought uncooperative, I am not preparing the statement you ask for'. He explained that '. . . the policy of the Department is to provide its services to everyone irrespective of race and, with a few minor exceptions (e.g. the provision of iron mixture for Maori babies to counter the widespread incidence of anaemia) this policy is rigidly adhered to. Because of statistically demonstrated differences in Maori-European standards of health, the Board of Health established a Maori Health Committee which, generally speaking, has not recommended the establishment of any special services for the Maori people. Your briefing therefore, does not have any special relevance in this context.'

Maori-pakeha relations

Throughout this paper, when reference is made to multi-racial policy, and to the requirements of New Zealanders of other than European descent, it is restricted mainly to consideration of the needs of the Maori people. They constitute, of course, the largest single group of citizens other than those of United Kingdom origin. The numbers of persons of Asian race are relatively small. Because entry into this country of persons of Asian origin has been carefully restricted, those that are resident here are, for the most part, industrious, law-abiding and reasonably prosperous. They therefore have little need of welfare services. There is a growing population of Pacific Islanders. Apart from the fact that these persons congregate in the cities, often in near sub-standard accommodation, and may require welfare services in an exclusively urban setting, there is little difference between their welfare needs and those of our Maori people. There will undoubtedly be an accelerating influx in the foreseeable future of other peoples if our country is to take its fair share of the world's population, but, so far, there are no welfare problems, on a significantly large scale, which are peculiar to races other than the pakeha and the Maori.

Welfare workers (whether they use that official designation or any other) have a significant part to play in preventing, forestalling or ameliorating the effects of racial disharmony. New Zealand is not exempt from the possibility of widespread racial strife. If regrettably, but not inconceivably, a demagogue or rabble-rouser should become established in a position of influence, he is most likely to come from the ranks of those who have personal grievances because they are in need of help and have not received it. He is unlikely to be a happy, well adjusted person. He could well be a malcontent with a genuine grievance. I believe therefore that every time a welfare worker does a successful job with a person of coloured ancestry needing help, he is removing a potential source of racial trouble. There may be an element of expediency and self-preservation in this, but there is mainly a basis of common humanity and common sense.

For this reason, it is essential that persons working in the welfare field should be free from racial prejudice. It goes almost without saying that no person is fitted to work in the welfare field if he or she chooses to regard a racial minority as *ipso facto* second-class citizens. No social worker worthy of the name would agree to a policy of apartheid which, whatever benefits it may be prepared to give to coloured persons, and whatever the intelligence or attainments or skills or conduct of those coloured persons, still chooses to regard them as inferior persons entitled to less than full citizenship. Any treatment imposed on the Maori people which isolated or segregated them or exposed them to any form of apartheid would be repugnant to the Maori people and would therefore be anathema to welfare workers. I have seen for myself most impressive work being done in the Government aboriginal settlements in the Northern Territory of Australia. No aboriginal is forced to go to the settlements or to remain there. First-class specialist services are available. The living conditions for the residents of the settlements are excellent and form an extreme contrast with the conditions under which aboriginals live elsewhere. The Commonwealth Government is clearly spending a lot of money on the settlements. Yet I believe that this form of welfare work, suited though it is to the needs of the aboriginal people of the Northern Territory, would be completely unacceptable to the Maori people, just as the reservations for the North American Indians would be. But it would be unrealistic to conclude from this that we have reached the stage in New Zealand where we can ignore the manifest differences in welfare needs between the Maori people and the pakeha.

The trend against discrimination

In this welfare state, while welfare services generally have been, and are, provided uniformly, irrespective of race, there have been, and are, exceptions to the general rule. Later in this paper I shall cite two instances where I believe the Maori people themselves have apparently advocated discrimination on racial grounds. Where discrimination has been practised on the initiative of the pakeha (and I am thinking particularly of Child Welfare matters), the explanation can be found not in a deliberate attitude of arrogance but, to the contrary, in a desire not to appear to be interfering with and upsetting the customs and ways of life of the Maori people. This could also explain why, with some services, the Maori people themselves had to seek the help available rather than have it offered to them.

During the depression years of the early 1930s, relief wages for those who would otherwise have been unemployed were paid at a lower scale to Maori workers (according to statements made in the House by the late Sir Eruera Tirikatene). Until fairly recently there were some differences in some Social Security benefits paid to Maori as compared with pakeha beneficiaries. In both cases the reasons advanced were usually that the needs of the Maori people were less because their living standards were lower. Whether this argument was right or wrong is only of historical interest now.

In the application of some other welfare policies, differences occurred. For instance, the Infant Life Protection provisions of the Infants Act 1908 were not formerly applied in the case of Maori children, because interference with Maori custom would have been resented and because of the difficulties of establishing what was the true family position in many cases. Then, too, Maori children were not admitted to special residential schools for special education as freely as the simple facts of the cases may have dictated. For instance, to take a retarded Maori boy from the bosom of his family at Te Hapua in the far North and admit him to Campbell Park School at Otekaike, near Kurow, half way down the South Island, would in most respects be an unwise move. The separation by such a long distance from his relatives could serve to build up a grievance likely to submerge any possible benefit to be derived from the residential special education available only in the South.

Further, Maori children living under conditions which, in the case of pakeha children, would have justified Court action leading to the children's committal to the care of the State, were often left undisturbed. This was partly because the end to be achieved would not in fact have been achieved, for a similar reason to the one given in the previous example. It was partly because of insufficient Child Welfare staff to cope with all the work the great number of cases of detrimental environment would have involved. It was also partly because there would have been an insuperable difficulty in placing all the Maori children who could justifiably have been removed from their homes. I recall an occasion years ago, when a newly appointed Magistrate, since deceased, who had lived a fairly sheltered life and who was presiding over a Children's Court, learned to his horror that a young Maori girl, appearing before him on a fairly minor charge of theft, was illegitimate and was living with her parents who still were not married. He promptly announced his intention of committing her to the care of the State in order to save her from the dreadful fate of living with parents who were *de facto* spouses. A wise and discreet woman Child Welfare Officer of long experience managed to get his attention quietly and to whisper to him, 'Your Worship, if all the children, Maori and pakeha, in this country who are living with unmarried parents are to be committed to the care of the State, it's not institutions or foster-homes we'll want; it's paddocks'. That story could well apply to the case of Maori children living under conditions which were sub-standard by pakeha criteria. The position does not apply today. With vastly improved housing standards, Maori families are now expected to face the legal consequences of failing to provide their children with the conditions to which all New Zealand children are entitled.

It so happens that preventive work with Maori families takes up a disproportionately high amount of the time of welfare workers, but there is nothing unusual or wrong about this. One would surely expect it. It is a welfare service's responsibility to be our brothers' keepers and a minority group emerging from backward conditions is surely entitled to an extra share of the time and skill made available by Government services.

Provision for special needs

Although welfare services are, generally speaking, administered today without discrimination on racial grounds, this does not rule out the circumstance that special consideration is given to the peculiar needs of racial groups. The main trend, however, is towards similar treatment for all.

Every country in the world has its lunatic fringe of people with a colour bias. New Zealand, I believe, has less than most. There are honest differences of opinion on how the welfare needs of the Maori people should be met, but I believe it would be both inaccurate and unfair to stigmatise as anti-Maori all those who oppose special provision for Maori people. There are many intelligent, kindly New Zealanders who believe in good faith that the best interests of the Maori people would be served by encouraging them to be independent, by refusing them so-called 'handouts', and by abolishing all apparent forms of discrimination in their favour. I do not agree with this attitude, but I respect it and I certainly do not regard it as evidence of colour prejudice.

I believe we pakeha New Zealanders have a continuing obligation to make a special effort, in our welfare requirements, to enable our Maori brethren to overcome the special disadvantages to which they are subject. Generally speaking they are not as articulate in the English language as we are. They have a different culture, different customs and a different background. Until recently their housing and general living conditions were markedly inferior to ours. They are still generally inferior, but not so markedly. These in turn, as R. J. Rose of the Medical Statistics Branch of the Department of Health has pointed out in his booklet *Maori-European Standards of Health,* have led to social inadequacies. R. J. Rose also makes the point that the higher accident rate among the Maori people is probably due to their being generally engaged in occupations giving less satisfaction. This not only causes more accidents, but it leads to an undue proportion of delinquency and crime, to more frequent neglect of children and to the cumulative effects of bringing families up in unhappy or unsatisfactory environments.

Because of these factors and because of our inherent obligation to the people whose land we took from them, I believe the Maori people should continue to enjoy any special privileges they have in the way of welfare services or in any other way (such as having Maori members of Parliament) for as long as they want them. It is for them to say when the privileges should end; not for us to decide when the need is no longer justified.

The Maori Welfare Division

The principal example of special or favoured welfare treatment of the Maori people is the existence of the Maori Welfare Division of the Department of Maori Affairs. The Maori people possess, through it, what is in practice a Citizens' Advice Bureau of which no counterpart is available to pakeha citizens. The multifarious range of functions of Maori Welfare Officers hardly qualifies them to become specialists in any one field. It does, however, encourage the Maori in need to turn to them for help in any problem at all. This requires the Maori Welfare Officer to be, in effect, a classifying agent, identifying the true nature of the problem and, in most cases, referring the client to the source which is best fitted to help him.

Some idea of the comprehensive assistance accorded to Maori people through their own welfare service can be gained from a reading of Section 18 (1) of the Maori Welfare Act 1962. Although the section particularly enumerates the general functions of the New Zealand Maori Council, I believe no words could describe better either the work of the Maori Welfare Officers, or the requirements of any welfare service for the minority racial group. The functions read:

(a) To consider and discuss such matters as appear relevant to the social and economic advancement of the Maori race:

(b) To consider and, as far as possible, give effect to any measures that will conserve and promote harmonious and friendly relations between members of the Maori race and other members of the community.

(c) To promote, encourage and assist Maoris—

(i) To conserve, improve, advance and maintain their physical, economic, industrial, educational, social, moral and spiritual well-being;

(ii) To assume and maintain self-reliance, thrift, pride of race, and such conduct as will be conducive to their general health and economic well-being;

(iii) To accept, enjoy and maintain the full rights, privileges and responsibilities of New Zealand citizenship;

(iv) To apply and maintain the maximum possible efficiency and responsibility in their local self-government and undertakings; and

(v) To preserve, revive and maintain the teaching of Maori arts, crafts, language, genealogy and history in order to perpetuate Maori culture.

(d) To collaborate with and assist State Departments and other organisations and agencies in—
  (i) The placement of Maoris in industry and other forms of employment;
  (ii) The education, vocational guidance and training of Maoris;
  (iii) The provision of housing and the improvement of the living conditions of Maoris;
  (iv) The promotion of health and sanitation amongst the Maori people;
  (v) The fostering of respect for the law and law-observance amongst the Maori people;
  (vi) The prevention of excessive drinking and other undesirable forms of conduct amongst the Maori people; and
  (vii) The assistance of Maoris in the solution of difficulties or personal problems.

The existence of the Maori Welfare Division makes all welfare services more easily accessible and acceptable to the Maori people than would otherwise be the case. It ensures that Maori people in need get the welfare service to which they are entitled, but of which they might not otherwise avail themselves because they were unaware of its existence. It allows service to be offered rather than sought. It makes it possible for the service to be given by the Maori people themselves or, if not by Maori people, by those pakeha staff members who have demonstrated their interest in and sympathy with Maori aspirations by identifying themselves with the work through obtaining employment as Maori Welfare Officers.

It has been said often enough that the main function of the Department of Maori Affairs is to be the architect of its own disappearance—that it should work towards the gradual absorption of its duties in other existing services catering for the whole community. While this may be a desirable long-term aim, there will, I believe, be a clear place in our society for a long time yet for the Maori Welfare Officer. Logically he may be obsolescent in a modern multi-racial society, but logic has no over-riding significance in social work. The alternative to retaining the Maori Welfare Division would not automatically be a more orderly administration of welfare services to the Maori people. It could well be resentment, deliberate refusal to use needed social services, embarrassment to the Government, and racial antagonism.

Multi-racial staffing

Other welfare services, notably vocational guidance, health, probation, and child welfare, have endeavoured with varying success to recruit suitably qualified or experienced Maori people into their work. It is essential that this process should continue, particularly having regard to the rate of increase of the Maori population. So far it has been disappointing to me personally, as the head of the Child Welfare Division, that we have been unable to attract more Maori applicants to jobs in our service, to hold those that we do appoint, and to promote, justifiably and fairly, to more senior positions, those who have remained in the service. It would surely not be too optimistic to think that there should be Maori people at the head of the Child Welfare service. There has been a Maori Minister of Health and there have been Maori persons in senior positions in other Government welfare services but, for some reason which I cannot find, the Child Welfare service has not had on its staff the proportion of Maori people which the population proportions and the nature of the job require.

Until recent years, it was our belief within the Child Welfare Division that immigrants of whatever race, with whatever qualifications, should not take up social work immediately on arrival in this country. We believed it was essential that the immigrant wishing to take up social work should first become acquainted with the customs and outlook of New Zealand people. Experience has shown that we were wrong in this belief. Lack of local knowledge has not been a handicap. Newcomers, even with language difficulties, have proved acceptable to the most aggressive and irrational of welfare clients, provided a love of people and a respect for human dignity are apparent from their general attitude. Admittedly what is sometimes a little difficult for experienced social workers from overseas to appreciate is the New Zealander's independence of outlook, his refusal to be pushed around or to accept too much in the way of directive counselling, and his ability to gain readily the ear of people in high places if he has a grievance. However, good social workers of all races are unlikely to give cause for complaint on the grounds of a dictatorial manner.

There is a belief which is hard to confute that Maori offenders appearing in Court suffer unduly because they are inarticulate and because Magistrates interpret this as indifference or arrogance or an admission of guilt. I do not accept the view that Magistrates do, in fact, act in this way. On the contrary, I believe they lean over backwards to be fair to the Maori offender. Similarly there is a fallacious argument to the effect that, in general, pakeha welfare officers completely misunderstand the Maori mind, boss their unresponsive Maori clients about, and arouse stubborn but inarticulate resentment. The exceptional cases where pakeha Welfare Officers act in this way are rare. The overwhelming majority of officers are only too keenly aware of the fact that, with Maori clients, they are dealing with people who need the most considerate and patient of treatment. They make allowances for differences of cultural background. They are anxious not to offend. In their anxiety they are more likely than otherwise to avoid taking the drastic action they would have taken had their clients been pakeha. In this the long-term interests of their clients may suffer. This is one of the reasons why a greater proportion of Maori people on the staffs of the welfare agencies would be desirable. Their presence would help to prevent clients developing imaginary grievances (which are real to themselves) and would help to educate their pakeha colleagues and give them more confidence in the handling of Maori cases.

Treating the Maori offender

A further argument to support the claim that more Maori staff should be working in other welfare agencies, as well as in the Department of Maori Affairs, could be made from the unduly high incidence of offending by Maori people. We are fond of saying that parents and other members of the public cannot avoid responsibility for the delinquencies not only of the young but also of the not so young. It is a community problem. If it is a community problem for everyone, then it is surely a community problem for the Maori people and they should be providing their fair share of persons prepared to work with offenders, both Maori and pakeha.

Welfare services in New Zealand include those concerned with young offenders. I am indebted to Mr Stuart Slater, the Research Officer to the Joint Committee on Young Offenders, for some facts about the position. He has given me statistics to show that in nearly all offence categories and age groups, Maori rates are two to three times as great as non-Maori rates. Maori offending at all ages, compared to non-Maori offending, is weighted slightly towards the less sophisticated property offences. Mr Slater adds, 'at present we probably know just as much about the causes of delinquency among Maori people as among non-Maori. What we take to be the obvious major cause—a family background which leads to a lowered efficiency and readiness to face life—seems to be the same for both groups; but Maori children are more often and more severely subject to such drawbacks than non-Maori children.' These few brief statements represent the pith of the matter, namely, that there is greater need for welfare services of a preventive nature among Maori people than among non-Maori. The handicaps of unsatisfactory living conditions, inadequate education and limited employment opportunities more commonly affect Maori youths than others. This has been generally recognised, and it would be unfair to minimise the substantial progress that has been made in recent years in the fields of housing, education, and vocational training and guidance for Maori youth.

In Child Welfare work the temptation is always present to take more drastic measures in dealing with a young Maori delinquent than with his pakeha counterpart. The home background of the Maori delinquent so often offers so little hope of preventive work succeeding that the welfare worker is inclined to favour the removal of the Maori child from his home to an entirely changed environment, often to an institution. It has been said, with some considerable evidence to support it, that the Maori youth conforms fairly readily to communal life in an institution and gives less trouble than his pakeha colleagues, but that the training and general life in the institution in the long run make no impression on him. He returns readily to his former habits of living and modes of conduct. I cannot pretend to know the answer to this problem. We are bound to continue to do the best we can, treating every case on its individual merits (and the merits include the circumstance that the offender is a member of the Maori race).

Reference to the problem, though, leads me to one of the examples of Maoris apparently favouring racial discrimination. Many of my Maori colleagues in social work favour the establishment of separate institutions for Maori offenders. They refer to both the traditional open-house Child Welfare institutions for delinquents and the secure penal institutions controlled by the Department of Justice. The argument is that the Maori offender would respond more readily to institutional treatment if he were segregated or associated or mixed (whichever word one chooses to use) with other offenders of his own race. I would not be foolish enough to regard this as a form of apartheid in reverse, any more than I would accept the suggestion that the existence of a New Zealand Maori fifteen was comparable with the existence of an All Black team from which Maori players were excluded. The latter is, for a number of reasons, a completely false analogy. The provision of institutions for Maori offenders only is, I am sure, not based on any thought that the presence of pakeha offenders would have a contaminating influence. Nor is it based on any suggestion that the Maori offender is likely to be less vicious than the pakeha offender. It is presumably based on the theory that a more effective and lasting response can be obtained if Maori offenders are dealt with by Maori methods. I doubt the efficacy of this and am more impressed by the argument that because the Maori offender, when he leaves the institution, will be living in a multi-racial society, he is better prepared for it if he is treated in a multi-racial institution. He cannot learn to live with his fellows by taking him away from contact with them. If it were so, then there would be a strong case for using solitary confinement for long periods for prisoners of any race. I do not agree with my Maori colleagues on the value of all-Maori institutions.

Adoption

The other example of apparent discrimination concerns the legal adoption of children. Before the Adoption Act of 1955 was introduced, the Government sought the advice of a committee of departmental representatives and private citizens experienced in the practice of adoption. The Committee was chaired by Mr S. T. Barnett, then Secretary for Justice. Among the members were Mr J. M. McEwen, now Secretary for Maori Affairs, and Mr C. M. Bennett, now Assistant Secretary for Maori Affairs. Because I too was a member, I can speak from personal knowledge of the fact that the Committee was strongly in favour of the abolition of any form of racial discrimination in adoptions. Prior to 1955 pakeha applicants could adopt a Maori child but Maori applicants could not adopt a pakeha child. Legal adoption of Maori children was rare, although the occasional order was made in the Maori Land Court. The overwhelming majority of Maori adoptions were by custom only. The Committee recommended that the restriction upon Maori applicants be abolished and the Government acted upon the recommendation. The Committee was anxious to encourage the gradual disappearance of the practice of adoption by custom, and its replacement by legal adoption. To require all Maori applicants to follow exactly the procedure recommended for other applicants would not have achieved this end. The Committee therefore recommended that Maori applicants be permitted to use the Maori Land Court rather than the Magistrate's Court, although an identical procedure would be used, qualified, of course, by the more informal atmosphere of the Maori Land Court. Express provision was recommended for Maori Welfare Officers to have the status of Child Welfare Officers for the purpose of reporting on adoption applications. Before the Committee submitted this recommendation to the Government, it consulted Mr T. T. Ropiha, then Secretary of Maori Affairs and himself a Maori, and gained his concurrence in the proposal. When the Government legislated in accordance with the recommendation, the Committee congratulated itself that, in a small way, it had contributed to the abolition of racial discrimination in adoptions, while at the same time permitting the Maori people to use their own Court and their own Welfare Officers.

The new Act generally worked well, despite the inexperience and occasional mistakes of Maori Welfare Officers in this new field. However, in 1962 the Government brought down an amendment removing adoption jurisdiction from the Maori Land Court and requiring Maori applicants to go in future to the Magistrate's Court. The move was made on the argument that this was a step forward in the abolition of racial discrimination. My personal opinion is that any racial discrimination in the use of the Maori Land Court was superficial rather than real and that the amendment was an oversimplified attempt (made of course in good faith) to deal with a complex problem. As far as I can judge, the passing of the 1962 Amendment has been disastrous. Legal adoptions by Maori applicants have fallen substantially (at a time when the total number of orders made has reached record levels) and adoption by custom, with all its unfortunate results for the children, has reverted to favour. The indications are that the Maori people themselves want to go back to the use of the Maori Land Court for adoption purposes. It would seem to me that they have merit in their desire, that a mistake has been made and that it could well be rectified. If the use of the Maori Land Court in preference to the Magistrate's Court is an example of racial discrimination, then this is one form of racial discrimination that I favour; but indeed I do not regard it as racial discrimination. As I said early in this paper, opposition to racial discrimination does not rule out the circumstance that special consideration should be given, in administering welfare services (and adoption is a welfare as well as a legal matter), to the peculiar needs of racial groups.

Cruelty to children

The desirability of avoiding the resurgence of adoption by custom and of facilitating legal adoption, highlights another welfare problem which has special significance for the Maori people. Physical cruelty to small children seems to be on the increase throughout the world. The 'battered baby syndrome', as it has come to be known, is causing concern to social workers everywhere. It is primarily, but not exclusively, one of the social problems of prosperity. In their innocence, humanitarians of all races once believed that, if the major scourges of poverty, illiteracy and disease could be defeated, little in the way of social problems would remain. Recent history has proved them wrong. In all the prosperous, industrially developed countries, where good education and health services are available to all, juvenile delinquency, mental ill health, emotional maladjustment and matrimonial problems are on the increase. So too is the incidence of cruelty to children. But it is not confined to any one race. Much sentimental nonsense has been written and said about Maori parents and parents of other coloured races being fonder of and kindlier to children than parents of European descent are. I believe that, in general, no race has a monopoly of fondness for children. Maori parents are generally no better and no worse than pakeha parents in their affectionate regard for their children. I say this despite what I have heard and read of a traditional Maori custom for the parents to concentrate their attention on the baby of the family and to leave the older children to look after the younger ones, other than the baby. However, perhaps because of a concentration of poorer living conditions, or perhaps because of the stresses produced from trying to compete with the more advanced standards of their neighbours when Maori people live in modern housing areas, there has been a disproportionate increase in cruelty to children by Maori adults. My authority for this statement is my own experience as head of the Child Welfare Division and the observations of officers of the Division who are reliable, have no axe to grind, and are free of racial prejudice. Statistics can refer only to convictions. Many cases of cruelty do not result in prosecution of those appearing to be responsible, even though they may result in drastic action in the interests of the victims. Even when prosecutions do result and even when cruelty is admitted, juries have a habit of acquitting the accused. There have been some dramatic, well-publicised examples of this in the recent past. I am convinced personally that there is a disturbingly high incidence of cruelty to small children by Maori adults. This calls, of course, for more intensive preventive welfare work by all relevant services, voluntary agencies as well as government administrations.

The role of voluntary agencies

A fear of those agencies which can and do exercise authority is one reason why so many inadequate citizens are suspicious of public servants exercising a welfare role. The voluntary social worker can therefore sometimes achieve a better rapport with those persons in need of welfare services. It is the job of the publicly administered welfare agencies, including the one in which I work, to ensure that all the available resources of the community are harnessed to deal with social problems. They should not confine themselves to the passive role of accepting assistance from the voluntary agencies when it is forthcoming. They should instead actively encourage and enlist the support— the mutual support—of statutory and voluntary agencies. I personally welcome the trend in recent years for Governments to provide substantial financial subsidies to voluntary welfare agencies so that those agencies are not forced to spend a disproportionate amount of their time on money-raising activities but can concentrate on improving their standards of work, as they clearly have done. For welfare requirements in a multi-racial society, strong and effective voluntary agencies are a prerequisite.

In addition to the agencies run under church control, the churches themselves can and do exert a considerable influence for good in furthering the welfare of minority racial groups. I would particularly single out the influence of churches such as the Mormon Church (of whose spiritual teachings I am ignorant, but whose moral teachings are self-evident) in countering the unfortunate tendency for many Maori people to indulge in excessive consumption of alcoholic liquor. It is unfortunately true that in multi-racial housing areas many Maori residents tend to get themselves branded as 'boozers'. The flagon has become a symbol of illusory good fellowship and has unfairly created a stigma which in turn creates bad feeling towards the Maori residents. As with my comments on cruelty to children, I cannot produce statistics to prove that the Maori citizen is a heavier drinker than his pakeha counterpart, but all my observations lead me to believe that he is.

I believe that a representative cross-section of welfare workers would confirm my belief that 'boozing' among Maori people contributes substantially to their social and welfare problems. I use the term 'boozing' deliberately. It is not a problem of alcoholism. It is a problem of drinking as a custom, copied to excess from the pakeha. The churches and the voluntary agencies can best handle this problem. The reintroduction of restrictive and discriminatory legislation on the sale of liquor to Maoris would not achieve any useful result. It is a hopeful sign that the Maori people themselves recognise the problem presented by excessive consumption of liquor and it is significant that a major part of the authority exercised by Maori Committees and Maori Wardens, under the provisions of the Maori Welfare Act 1962, is concerned with conduct arising out of drunkenness.

The natural dignity of the Maori people is not enhanced by those of its representatives who set a bad example of excessive drinking, nor is it helped by those Maori entertainers who set out to raise laughs by self-denigratory jokes of the 'Nigger Minstrel', 'Black Sambo' type. There is little that welfare agencies can do to counter the effects of this, except to decline to perpetuate the jokes.

When one considers the sum of the efforts made by many people over a long time to promote the welfare of the Maori people and then considers the failure of a conspicuous minority of them to help themselves, one wonders whether there would be merit sometimes in playing down the help that Maori people should get and in emphasising the ways in which they can help other less fortunate peoples. It is a salutary lesson for anyone with a grievance to realise that others are worse off. To be concerned about the needs of others can serve to put one's own problems in their rightful place. I have no doubt that Maori citizens contribute, like other citizens, to appeals such as those made by CORSO, for the relief of distress in starvation areas overseas. I wonder whether their own welfare would be promoted if greater attention were given by Maori groups to those in need elsewhere in the world. Charity certainly begins at home, but if it ends there, it creates selfishness and an undue preoccupation with domestic grievances. I say that, with no malice towards my

Maori brethren, and with no intention of indulging in the luxury of a homily. It is not part of the job of a welfare worker, whether he be a top administrator or a subordinate officer well down the line, to tell a whole race of people how it should conduct itself, any more than it is the prerogative of a welfare agency to promote or oppose integration. It is simply the job of welfare workers to help individual people in need.

Coordination of services

The inter-relationship of various welfare agencies is a matter for constant debate in any society, multi-racial or otherwise, but is of particular concern in a multi-racial society because of the greater possibilities of confusion arising. Overlapping and duplication occur in New Zealand welfare services, even if not to the exaggerated extent claimed by some advocates for one comprehensive all-embracing welfare service. No one would advocate that representatives from five or six welfare agencies should separately call on the one client. Nevertheless, if specialist services are to be rendered, sometimes this is justifiable. The alternative would be for second-rate help or advice to be rendered by one officer who would face the well-nigh impossible task of being a specialist in five or six fields. It is conceivable, but unlikely, that one officer could at the same time be a psychiatrist, a physician, a psychologist, a housing expert, a Child Welfare Officer, a visiting teacher, and a Social Security social worker. It is true that today all welfare agencies are aware of the effect that a succession of visits by experts can have on a family in need, and a conscious effort is made to avoid any suggestion of 'passing the buck'. There is better coordination than ever before between welfare agencies. A start has been made on the grouping of individual welfare services under the one roof. This should lead to the kind of classifying and referring that is already done for the Maori people by the Maori Welfare Officers. In other words, it could lead to the establishment of Citizens' Advice Bureaux, whether they were called by that name or not.

Ever since there have been welfare agencies in New Zealand there has been a running debate on the merits of forming one comprehensive department of social welfare. I suppose it is inevitable that some such department will eventually be established but it would be foolish to presume that such a change would necessarily solve the problem of a succession of callers on one family. A department of social welfare would be made up of specialists in various fields. Some client families would need the services of several specialists. However, the fusion of various welfare agencies into one whole would certainly make easier for members of minority racial groups the search for adequate welfare aid. A person, particularly with a coloured skin, may feel resentment towards all authority, may feel inferiority or may be arrogant, may feel inadequate or merely different. An initial approach to the wrong quarter for welfare aid may be his last approach. He could well be reluctant to risk a second mistake and become disgruntled. Such a person should be treated with special tact. The existence of a single centre where his wants may be properly identified and promptly attended to would facilitate successful treatment from the time he first seeks help.

The administrator of a welfare agency should not restrict his thinking about coordination to consideration of how his agency can best cooperate with other welfare agencies clearly defined as such. He should also seek to exert an influence on other fringe agencies by accepting membership of inter-departmental and other coordinating committees where the requirements of social services can easily be overlooked and should be stressed. More so in the past than now, welfare work has been regarded as something fairly remote, as acts of charity which can be praised when they come to notice but which are concerned with a tiny, almost unknown section of the community. Any extension of welfare services was apt to be regarded as a luxury. The climate has changed today. There is now general recognition, first, that if we are to have a healthy society in the future we must have adequate social services today, and second, that no citizen is exempt from the possibility that he and his family will need the services of a welfare agency. Despite this recognition, there is still a need for the voice of the welfare administrator to be heard when such fringe matters as town planning, national expenditure, school curricula, public works projects, human rights as affected by the administration of criminal justice, and civil defence are being discussed. The proper recognition today of the place occupied by efficient social services is due to the circumstance that some welfare administrators have made it their business to ensure, by astute campaigning in the right quarters, that social service agencies are given seats at the table when important national or civic deliberations are taking place. This recognition could easily be lost by default if social welfare administrators retire to their ivory towers and do not take the initiative in mixing in the general fray. Because the need for welfare services will undoubtedly increase as New Zealand becomes more and more of a multi-racial state, as it assuredly will do, so too the need for welfare agencies to get their fair share of available funds and staff and facilities will have to be continually established. The day never dawns when one can say that the battle has been won.

Conditions for efficiency

The reader may well wonder at this stage when I am going to relate my comments specifically to the subject of welfare requirements in a multi-racial society. I would hope that some of the requirements have emerged from the comments I have freely offered on a number of topics. For the rest, I would say that the requirements are similar to those of any public welfare agency in any well developed society, regardless of whether it is multi-racial or not. Having seen welfare agencies in the United States, where, because of the fetish for local control and local financing, wealthy communities have excellent agencies, and poor communities, where the need is greatest, have poor agencies or none at all, I am strongly in favour of the national, rather than local or regional, organisation of public welfare agencies. This ensures national coverage and reasonable uniformity of service. The citizen in the most rural areas should have access to roughly the same service as the citizen in the capital city receives. The same overall policy, subject to the exercise of individual discretion in the merits of individual cases, should prevail. Staff should enjoy good working conditions and should receive adequate training. Staff morale should be kept at a high level by developing a good system of communication and consultation within the agency, so that every officer, whatever his level, can feel that he is contributing to the development of the service and is part of a going concern. It is easy for a welfare worker, particularly if he is working in a fairly remote area, to lose heart and to be affected detrimentally by the cases of his clients. It is the job of an administrator to guard against this. The retention of high morale among staff, the constant injection of a spirit of adventure into the work and the encouragement of constructive ideas are all essential aspects of his responsibility. The day of the good-hearted muddler in social work has long gone. Social services today must be efficient. Social workers being the kind of people that they are, efficiency is not to be achieved entirely by discipline from the top. It requires the active and willing cooperation of everyone in the social service, including those playing an ancillary role as basic-grade clerks, typists, gardeners, and domestics.

Conclusion

To sum up, what I have tried to show is:

(1) That New Zealand is openly and unashamedly a welfare state, in which the Government maintains certain welfare services which I have identified.

(2) Those welfare services are available to all, regardless of race.

(3) The multi-racial society in New Zealand is principally made up of persons of European and of Maori descent.

(4) While there is no discrimination on racial grounds, the peculiar needs of racial groups may justify special consideration; specifically, welfare services in New Zealand have an obligation to help our Maori people to overcome their handicaps in competing with Europeans in a modern society.

(5) The Maori Welfare Division, as a classifying and referring agency in the main, fulfils the role of a Citizens' Advice Bureau and thus enables the Maori people to avail themselves of welfare services of which they might otherwise be unaware.

(6) It is a welfare agency's first job to give help where it is needed, not to promote or oppose any overall policy of integration.

(7) Welfare employees should be free of racial prejudice and welfare agencies should for preference have a multi-racial staff.

(8) Voluntary welfare agencies should be encouraged, with Government financial help, partly because they do not represent authority to the Maori people.

(9) The welfare agencies play a significant role in promoting racial harmony because the trouble-making demagogue is likely to be one who needs, but has failed to receive, their services.

(10) The disproportionate incidence of delinquency, crime, ill treatment of children, and drunkenness among the Maori people justifies their receiving a disproportionate share of the attention of welfare services, especially in preventive work.

(11) Adoption procedures should recognise the special needs of the Maori people by reverting to use of the Maori Land Court.

(12) Welfare administrators should ensure that their voices are heard in 'fringe' areas of policy and administration which have indirect relevance to welfare.

(13) Welfare services should be efficient and better coordinated, not playthings of well-intentioned muddlers, but always remembering that human beings in need (particularly among minority racial groups) are creatures of emotion, for which full allowance should be made.

Planning   Problems
Prespectives

J. E. RITCHIE

History finished yesterday. Politics begins today and its concern is tomorrow. Just as history becomes less determinate in direct proportion to the distance back in time from yesterday, so politics becomes less determinate the further ahead we make the reach and the goal of our planning. It is as rash to assign some final future fate for the Maori minority in New Zealand as it is to decide at this stage what their historical origins may have been. The more knowledgeable one is concerning either of them, the better one's guess, and politicians can, I suppose, deal in part with unsupported guesses, but not administrators: their guesses must have more solid probability values. So the administrator, as I understand the matter, works closer to what is than to what should be, unless the 'should be' is unequivocally indicated. Such indication may be of two kinds. Either policy may be based on nationally acceptable principles of an ethical or normative kind, or it must be backed by uncontrovertible, though sometimes very abstract, fact. In inter-ethnic affairs the first guide is clear enough but the second is less determined.

The facts presented in this series of papers indicate that we are a nation of mixed ethnic identification and background. They also indicate that such groups have been and will continue to be a feature of our society for sufficient time ahead to require that firm policy be formulated. But they also indicate the need for flexibility in any policy made or adopted. Furthermore the diversity of such groups and the range of possible developments within and between them make it questionable whether we can have one overall policy concerning minorities or whether we need alternatives within policies, as well as overriding principles. A complex society may require more than the narrow application of a single policy principle. Or to put the matter another way: overall policy in an integrated society may demand a variety of sub-policies each matched to particular groups, sub-groups and circumstances. The facts we have been considering are just facts; they speak with only a muted voice if we ask them to predict their own trend lines, and they are utterly silent if we ask them to say what we as a nation should do.

Mr Mardle asks that we shake off our preoccupation with the present; that we recognise from the present and the obvious trend lines of the future that we are a society of ethnic diversity and will become more so; he reminds us that the emotional, psychological and economic conflicts arising from ethnic diversity are far from being resolved under present policy and administrative measures. I could not agree more. Vision and a sense of direction are essential administrative qualities. But the overall impression with which we are left is, that present policies have been working rather well for the things they have been attempting to do, that the enormous changes of the last 20 years have not left us with a seriously increased measure of disruption or left us dismayed, that the attitudes of the majority are still only latently and minimally prejudicial towards ethnic minorities. Indeed, compared with either our own recent past or with situations more nearly comparable in other countries, New Zealand today is not such a very bad place for a member of some minority group to be in. The social climate into which a Maori migrating to a town arrives is one of considerable opportunity; indeed the openness of that society is by far the greatest of the problems he must face.

Mr Bradly reports on an educational structure which is also managing to deal with minorities, on the whole, rather well. Where it is deficient, it is generally so. Poor provision for pre-school services, guidance counselling, inadequate specialist services for those with some educational handicap or special need, for the education of the gifted, the almost total lack of attack on the problem of what should constitute a general non-academic education, the problem of non-academic goals for the non-academic pupil, residential provision for secondary pupils of rural origin; all these constitute general problems in which the provision is equally poor for the minority as for the majority population, though the effect on minorities may be greater and more tragic. But the deficiencies of the system are not ones of which administration is unaware. Nor is it totally inactive on these issues, merely lethargic.

Mr McEwen and Mr Anderson both show the pragmatic steady wisdom which is characteristic of the best policy-making in this country. Both, it seems to me, are carefully judging the balance between what can be achieved by the staff and structure at their disposal and what is best in the national interest. Neither seems over-persuaded by theorising, and rightly so, for in the area of social planning, theory can be only a very general guide. Nigel Balchin once wrote that 'All the worst crimes in history were committed by men who passionately believed in their own rightness'. I doubt that we shall see many administrative crimes in either of these two Departments.

Dr Metge with her usual precise and careful attention to words and how we should use them, presents us with some seemingly clear policy alternatives. While the distinctions clarify thinking they should all be kept in mind as alternatives which may in some circumstances be administratively justified. Even segregation may have its place where a *cordon sanitaire* is required.

Through these papers there runs, if I interpret the authors correctly, a general theme of what might seem to be self-congratulation, but is better interpreted as an expression of a national sense of assurance that we can handle minority groups capably within our present administration and that we shall go on doing so. What is not so clear and what becomes, therefore, our closing task, is the definition of how these policies might evolve and the question of their overall adequacy for the future, or that small part of it which we can with confidence predict.

In considering how administration directly influences the ethnic minorities in our midst, a central set of questions arises. Can present policies in diverse Departments be subsumed under a general policy of the kind of which Dr Metge writes or must the policies necessarily differ? If so, on what grounds is such difference based? Do those Departments which deal with several minorities have differing policies for each? Does any one Department have a different policy basis for different sections or aspects of life within some particular minority?

The policy of integration elaborated in the Hunn Report[1] and subsequently by Hunn and Booth[2] was clearly stated to apply to Maori and pakeha society, individuals and culture. To the extent that it was adopted as Government policy, it presumably also applied wherever administrative action in any Department was concerned with Maori-pakeha relations or with Maori clients. I say Maori clients because we do not have a Department of Pakeha Affairs. Whether this policy was ever intended to apply to Dutch or Hungarian immigrants was never, to my knowledge, discussed. The policy also extended to people of Polynesian origin generally, though its application is more dubious for them since they start, in the case of some groups, with the assets of more intact tribal attitudes, loyalties and kinship and with the liabilities of lesser knowledge of the diversity and perversities and complexities of our society. Therefore, the autonomy and responsibility for individual decision-making which integration implies may be less appropriate and a policy of building or strengthening group identification and social functioning may possibly require more intervention even at the risk of appearing to act with paternalism.

What we need to know, concerning the policy alternatives Dr Metge places before us, is where and when and for whom each is indicated. Another consequent question is this: at what stage can a minority be expected to pass from one alternative policy to another, what is the sequential (if any) arrangement of the alternatives she presents? Are there some areas of Maori life where integration is an immediate prospect and others where cultural pluralism is more desirable? Are there some Maoris who, as Ernest Beaglehole was repeatedly pointing out, seem to have passed a point of cultural no return, who no longer possess enough working contact with, or command of, Maori culture and who, therefore, must be considered under the policy alternative of assimilation? And if there are, how do we recognise them? Does this mean that the Department of Maori Affairs should have two parallel policies to deal with two kinds of Maoris or should these be considered more as end-on alternatives for the Department as Hunn suggested? His Report, you may remember, indicates that integration as policy would not prevent assimilation, might even

[1] J. K. Hunn, *Report on the Department of Maori Affairs*, Government Printer, 1960.
[2] J. M. Booth and J. K. Hunn, *Integration of Maori and Pakeha*, Special Studies Series No. 1. Department of Maori Affairs. Government Printer, Wellington, 1962.

aid and give way eventually to it and in this the deep suspicion with which some Maoris greeted it may be justified.

While I am on this subject I must confess some bewilderment at Dr Metge's suggestion that any of her alternatives could be adopted by an administration as a 'final state, the completion of the process' of inter-ethnic contact. None of them seems to me to be this. Indeed, the idea that any social process can have a final end state seems not just anathema to me but quite inconceivable. Policy based on some final point may be all very well if you want to tear up a railway or stop building a cotton mill; though I wonder even here if the apparent finality is a truly political and social finality. We are not, fortunately, likely to find a policy alternative in practical politics which will provide the 'final solution' to the 'Maori problem'.

Integration as a concept seems to me to be reaching the point where it has become adopted as a clear and positive policy alternative to the exclusion of other possibilities. It clearly has many points to recommend it. It is a process term for continuing social accommodations between ethnic groups. The community (or at least its better informed members) has come to have a conception of it that is reasonably close to that which the policy-makers intended. It has been adopted internationally as the most favoured policy for 'governments and experts charged with the task of improving the social and living standards of indigenous peoples in metropolitan communities'.[3] It is free of paternalist implications and does not contravene our kind of democratic system. It is modern, urban and industrial in its implications. It is, furthermore, capable of serving as an overall policy for any number of different minorities even though the degree of readiness for various steps or stages in integration may vary from group to group. It can cover differing degrees of readiness to change within various parts of the life of or the personnel of any one group. Its supreme virtue, ironically, is that it doesn't tell administrators what to do in an automatic or cook-book way, but enables decisions to be made about different aspects of living in different ways. It has, therefore, great flexibility, but poor directive definition. It implies that fusion may be possible in some areas immediately, or that accommodation (a term which I add to Dr Metge's list: that graceful process of mutual changes between people of good will who

---

[3] See Beaglehole, E., *The Process of Integration.* International Labour Office. Geneva.

want to understand and appreciate each other) can take place. It stands in sharp contrast to segregation. It permits pluralism. My chief worries are that it may lack definition to the point where the administrator is unable to make clear decisions in terms of it and that it may have been adopted to the exclusion of other alternatives.

Better definition, it seems to me, can be given if we consider this policy alternative in the light of social evolution as a total process[4] and couple with it the general idea of readiness, and of other policy alternatives in special circumstances. All over the world accelerated rates of social change are occurring and in a much more orderly way, given an evolutionary perspective, than most people think. We used to talk of the folk-urban continuum, a rather primitive conception in itself since it focused on the act of migration and emphasised the sociology of change rather than matters of attitude and sentiment or total way of life. Nowadays, the growing sophistication within the study of social change draws the contrast more between peasant and industrial civilisation. And everywhere the peasant is on the way out. No one really seems to want to keep the peasant values intact, least of all the peasants themselves. No one wants to deny himself the material advantages of modern industrial civilisation, nor the social advantages of greater freedom and autonomy that go with it, nor its possibility for greater education and knowledge, of greater environmental mastery and a richer and more varied recreational and aesthetic experience. To make the act of translation to the industrial social modality some things must go. The extended family is one. An economy of kinship reciprocity is another. Bloodline leadership a third. Some sociologists have even suggested that monogamy itself is being supplanted by serial polygamy in the modern industrial environment, though this, to me, is going too far. The tribe as a controlling point of reference for the individual cannot survive the change and is most frequently replaced by a broader ethnic identification. Tribal economics are dead. The tribal family is dead. Even the tribal idea of God is dead.

The idea that these changes must take place slowly is itself a piece of tribal thinking as is the material determinist fallacy that, to quote Dr Metge, 'culture change proceeds from material goods to

4 For an extended discussion of the concept of cultural evolution, see Mead, M., *Continuities in Cultural Evolution,* Yale University Press, New Haven, 1964.

ideas'. Most of history denies this, quite apart from current instances. Martin Luther was not reacting to a new rosary, a re-
arrangement of the votive candles or extra hair in his habit. Ideas
and particularly the release of creativity within a culture which
the new challenge of opportunity may make possible produce the
most potent widespreading and revitalising changes in culture.
James Baldwin presents to the American negro a new conception
of being negro in America and not just because he has a new
fountain pen.

We earnestly need this kind of perspective. Modern industrial
society provides a bewildering range of possibilities to the eman-
cipated peasant and at the same time sternly requires certain
things of him. You will not stop people from wanting to be and to
feel modern, and no one would want to. But what must be defined
are the things that industrial civilisation requires and then efficient
ways must be devised to provide a rapid approximation to these
basic requirements. Thereafter, in an integrated society, what a
man does is his own affair.

At the present time, policy does seem to be most effective at the
level of socio-economic change and least effective when it concerns
itself with the total quality of life in the new situation. It is quite
untrue to assume that new houses, new appliances and a steady
wage are enough to guarantee integrated adjustment. We must add
to the minimal list of things required some which are less tangible
but much greater and more important sources of satisfaction.

It seems to me that the minimum list should include these
things: a mastery of the dominant language, literacy in it, a desire
to achieve in the new environment, commitment to the development of the full education potential of one's children, a minimal
command of the savings-credit system of finance, a willingness to
enter into, and accept, responsibility in neighbourhood and other
voluntary associations, acceptance of the time-equals-money-
equals-work ethos, voting responsibility, and with it the desire and
the confidence to make one's opinion heard. Some change in the
status of women and the care of children may be necessary too,
but of this I am less sure.

At the same time one could write a list of those things which
seem to impede urban and industrial adjustment, things that stem
from the peasant view of the world. But this list, because it must
have its origin in the cultures from which people have come,
rather than where they are going, needs to be specified for each
particular cultural or ethnic group.

Other things follow. The loss of indigenous culture is not imperative. But it is a danger and very likely unless those who make policy are aware of the psychological necessity of sure cultural foundations. Some of the things kinship and the tribal community did for the individual, both tangible things like help in times of tragedy, death or disturbance, and less tangible things like psychological security, will not be automatically replaced in the urban-industrial complex. Indeed psychological security (as against material security) is rather poorly provided for all who live in modern cities. Hence the need not only for welfare services, but also for the examination of what 'community' means in an urban civilisation and how it can better function, for community carries and creates culture. What is to replace a peasant background of reciprocity on the basis of kinship or the control over the young by community scrutiny, or indeed over everyone by the sanctions of gossip where nothing can be hidden because everything is public? In these matters we are doing virtually nothing and the model of the Maori Welfare Officer who is both a resource man for people in trouble and a real community worker is one which bears careful examination and possible extension into the wider community.

As we look at our own society, who within it is still remote, who, untouched by the urban industrial nature of our way of life? Not only have our cities grown in themselves, but their influence has reached back into the hinterlands till all New Zealand can be thought of as inter-connected—one big city—or as one sometimes thinks, one big village.

So far we have extended the policy of integration to the easiest things on my list, which are also, not without reason, the things which can most readily display objective evidence that the policy works. They make a good showing at the hustings, not to mention at United Nations. We have handled piecemeal, but well, some of the deficiency problems, assistance with re-housing has been provided, trade-training schemes put into operation, health measures legislated and services provided, welfare services as a rescue measure built up, even some anticipatory welfare preparations to prevent the need for rescue. We are belatedly getting into a higher gear on educational provisions, though the gap between what is provided and what the major minority, the Maori people, want right now, is in danger of turning sour the cream of enthusiasm so obvious to those in contact with Maori local opinion.

In the Maori field we have continued to make solid progress in the yielding problems that Ngata and the Young Maori Party began to tackle in the early part of this century, though some, like Maori land tenure, were not and are not, we can now see, as yielding as we thought and this is because we attended to their legal or economic aspects rather than to the social or cultural. The difficult things remain and though we may worry about them from time to time, either they seem beyond the scope of the kind of administration we have constructed, or we leave them for solution by the minority themselves, disregarding the likelihood that what proves to be beyond the capacity of a trained and skilled administrator is unlikely to yield to the efforts of the minority themselves.

Rising crime rates amongst Maoris are a case in point. The best efforts of administration have not stemmed this. The interminable discussions at Maori gatherings have done little except to make Maoris feel incompetent and somehow responsible, in ways they cannot clearly understand, for something they are powerless to control.

This has led some to take the view that crime and similar social disruption is a built-in price which must be paid for the advantages of urban industrial participation; to take the view that Maori crime is a product of a transient situation which will become worse before it becomes better, but that it will become better sooner or later. This view is, I know, very prevalent amongst those who have most intimate contact with Maori offenders, but it is irrational and over-sanguine, expressing at best a pious hope and at worst, a cynicism which has no place in the agencies of a welfare state.

We know a great deal about the causes of crime and much of what we do know has direct application to the minority group situation in New Zealand. I doubt that causes themselves need much more pure research at this stage. Similarly, we know a lot about educational handicap amongst minority groups in general, sufficient to suggest that in the case of both these problems applied research, action research, is what is really indicated. Sufficient is known about causes to enable the planning of possible cures or preventive measures, but little is known about which possibilities might work and which will work best. We can probably best further our understanding of causes by examining pragmatic cures and seeking to understand why they are effective, assuming that we are clever and imaginative enough to find some that do work. This is the sort of proposal that the University of Waikato is seeking to put into operation through its Maori Research Centre while at the same time holding to the University function of seeking truth and knowledge beyond the merely pragmatic.

But as you examine any problem area, be it crime, educational disadvantage or land complexities, one thing stands out with increasing clarity. All these problems inter-relate. And from the realisation of this, two challenges emerge. One is the question of how to relate one part of administrative action to another so that the inter-relation of problems can be more comprehensively managed. The other is that they inter-relate within groups who not so long ago had a peasant community background and all that this implies, and who still have a symbolic community of interest as well as a real community with structure and function.

Let us tackle the latter of these two and then proceed to the other. Some hold the view that the warm grasp of the tribal community is kinship-based and has been moulded during centuries of pragmatic social and cultural decision-making. Further, they assert that once broken, this embrace cannot be renewed and the individual must learn to live in the relative loneliness of the city. Others hold that the 'little community' concept can survive if we work to make it function in the urban situation. The first view is probably correct and the second of particular but highly limited application; and the risks of segregation or of ghetto formation must be kept in mind. Both must be put against the clear evidence that new kinds of community develop in cities, looser perhaps, in some cases wider, defined by common association and common interest rather than by kinship, and they carry and create new forms of the old culture. The health of our city population, indeed, of our civilisation, depends on the rapid solution to the problem of defining what community means in an urban setting, for all who live there, and directing administration towards the efficient operation of urban community life. Here we vitally need more sociological research to tell us what the urban community is like, in human and social terms, so that we can find ways of replacing the functions which peasant community served by appropriate community functions in the city. We are all strangers in the urban jungle which we have created but only poorly control, and we cannot afford the structure of administration that would be needed if all the old functions of the community, particularly its welfare functions, were to be borne by the State. Along with research on the urban community as a whole we need to relocate and restructure our services to serve the functioning communities rather than the abstract community. Our greatest administrative deficiency is the divorce, sometimes almost total, between services and locality or other defined community groups.

It is here that the broad functions of the Maori Welfare Officer have so exemplary a role. Viewed from one aspect, he carries the burden of everything and the load seems impossible. But in the field he can deal, as no other agency can, with the community (and it really isn't a peasant community any more even in the most remote parts of New Zealand). He is intuitively working, perhaps even without awareness that he is doing so, on a process of directed community change. He is one administrative answer to the inter-relation of social problems and he is most effective when he can work through communities to which the problems relate. On the other hand, the Child Welfare Officer is engaged, for the most part, in individual case work, and cannot concern himself with the social health of the community that produced the family that bore the child whose problem is the officer's concern.

The trend line in Maori Affairs indicates that the welfare functions will expand further with increasing population and urbanisation. The Maori Welfare Officer has been most effective in the rural areas and there is a danger that he might interpret his urban function in the same way as a Child Welfare Officer, to do individual casework because he sees no community like the rural ones with which to work. This seems to me to be one clear challenge to administration. Minority groups need community welfare workers. Indeed our society as a whole needs them. They could be trained and provided with an administrative framework within which to work, but there is no present provision for either.

Let us summarise my argument. Of the minority groups in New Zealand, only those who directly immigrate from remote Pacific islands have a truly peasant experience. Since they, and we, know what they moved from, we can see their problems clearly and schedule the sub-goals of integration accordingly. Since they are so obviously incapacitated by their entry to the urban-industrial nature of New Zealand culture we attend to their needs and they want and accept our help. They carry with them, for as long as they need it, the image of the peasant community. But for minorities well along the highway of integration, the goals are less clear and the peasant-like idea of community is impractical however romantically it may be desired. While we have built up administrative machinery to handle specific problems and meet specific adjustment needs, we have not in the past considered it wise to help people re-define their culture in the new setting and build up a new sense of community; not, I hasten to add, community apart from, but within that awful remote abstraction, the wider community. We have allowed disintegration, concerned ourselves only with its problem aspects and not with its creative possibilities. We need to consider the process of integration within the context of the evolutionary development of an urban industrial complex and ask ourselves what administrative policy can do to help people create out of disruption, to sense the delight of taking up the opportunity to construct within their cultural tradition new and satisfying ways of living and new ways of effective community.

The future of minorities lies within the urban-industrial complex and in urban-industrial communities. The realistic acceptance of this premise implies a reassessment of the policies governing Maori Affairs and Island Territories. Somewhere we must make provision for the welfare needs of islanders in New Zealand. Relocation residences must be provided both for families and for young people. City community centres set up. City marae facilities established. The specific short-term adjustment courses of trade-training and for city employment could be extended and should be. There have long been possibilities of providing more trade-training in rural areas where industry exists, Kawerau for example, which have not been exploited. Decentralisation of industry could increase these possibilities though the economics of this are the crucial limiting factor.

We cannot hand crime control, drug addiction, illegitimacy and similar problems back to a community unless one exists. We cannot afford to expand the State welfare system indefinitely in order to replace community responsibility for social problems and social welfare. It seems to me, therefore, clear that we must use our welfare resources to create communities, to strengthen them and then to transfer to them the responsibility of social action to resolve social problems. Proto-communities have emerged, Ngati Poneke, Ngati Akarana, Ngati Hamutana, and old indigenous communities exist also, Orakei, Takapuwahia Pa at Porirua, the Petone people at Tatou-o-te-po, and one could proliferate examples. But they are not strong and we are doing little to strengthen them. A policy of integration does not say that we should not do so—rather to work it says that we must.

If we are to overcome the difficulties in administering an inter-ethnic society, then we must think more clearly and creatively about the inter-relation of administrative functions themselves which the Cabinet system puts apart and no man seems able to draw together.

This problem was the central theme of the Institute's conference a few years ago when the need for integration within welfare services was discussed.[5] Mr Bradly gives an urban example of this need when he cites schools of very mixed ethnic composition. Another example is the divided educational responsibility between Maori Welfare Officers, Child Welfare Officers and other parts of the Education Department's administration. A Pa close to a small rural community not far from my University has been the subject of reports to Head Offices by the head teacher, the District Health Nurse, the Maori Welfare Section, Child Welfare and perhaps a number of other agencies. These result in committee discussions but what the community really needs is a resident community welfare worker. The present procedures emphasise the Maori aspects of what are really problems of the whole community. Present administrative methods are too remote and too partial to promote community health in its widest sense in this case. There must be many others like it.

We must also attend far more to the recreational and aesthetic needs of those for whose welfare we administer. We must think in terms of urban communities defined not by a geographic boundary but by the motor car and all that it makes possible. We must provide facilities or help people provide their own facilities to increase the possibilities of creating within the urban community all those things which are most humanly satisfying. We must help people connect together into groups that will care for their members and then we must help them in their caring, the better to receive the migrant, celebrate a birth, or a marriage, or the rehabilitation of some member or the death of anyone connected within the community of concern. Some will not be responsive to this challenge but we cannot know how many until the alternative is realistically presented. Those who then reject it will be neither

---

[5] ed. Scott, K. J., *Welfare in New Zealand,* N.Z. Institute of Public Administration and Oxford University Press, 1955.

worse nor better off than they are now. My guess is that sufficient will be responsive to make the effort worth while. If politics is the art of the possible then it will achieve its highest expression when it attacks those problems which are by no means easy but which are likely to be of the greatest long-term benefit.

Appendices

CROSS-CULTURAL PROBLEMS IN SOCIAL SECURITY

It should be remembered that the main objective of social security in New Zealand is to provide income security for the *whole* population against loss of income or reduction below the minimum needed for subsistence, and this provision is not restricted to certain groups within the community on grounds of race or nationality.

Functions of Social Security

A brief summary of the functions of the Social Security Department is as follows:

Social Security cash benefits.

War pensions and allowances—medical treatment—other related matters.

Supplementary assistance and war pensions supplementary assistance.

Capitalisation of family benefit.

Rehabilitation of ex-servicemen.

Social work service and allied welfare services.

Pensions and other payments in New Zealand on behalf of overseas Governments or other overseas authorities.

These services are available to all persons regardless of race, but some immigrant groups may not qualify for some benefits on grounds of residence.

Cash Benefits

The cash benefits paid in New Zealand are:

(a) *Benefits in respect of age:* Superannuation benefit provides a non-means-test benefit based on age 65 years and 20 years' residence in New Zealand; age benefits are subject to an income test and are based on age 60 years and 20 years' residence in New Zealand. For persons in New Zealand on 15 March 1938 only 10 years' residence is required for both age and superannuation benefits.

(b) *Loss of breadwinner:* Widows' benefits, deserted wives' benefits and special benefits for wives of mental patients are all subject to an income test and to residential and other qualifications which are the same for all racial groups. Orphans' benefits are available subject to birth of the child in New Zealand or three years' New Zealand residence of parents immediately preceding death.

(c) *Permanent cessation of employment owing to ill health:* Invalids' benefits subject to an income test are based on total blindness or permanent incapacity for work and require 10 years' residence in New Zealand. Non-means-test miners' benefits are for miners suffering from occupational disease and require five years' New Zealand residence and 2½ years in mining employment.

(d) *Temporary cessation or reduction of income:* Sickness benefits provide help for persons over age 16 years, subject to an income test, medical certification and 12 months' residence in New Zealand; unemployment benefits are available under similar conditions except that unemployment is the main qualification.

(e) *Family Benefits:* These are payable for each child in the family and require 12 months' New Zealand residence. The benefit may be capitalised to build a house, buy a new house not previously occupied, buy a house from the Crown, buy a section and build a house on it, make alterations or additions to a house already owned, or to repay debts on a home under certain circumstances.

(f) *Reciprocity:* Agreements exist between New Zealand and Australia and the United Kingdom for reciprocal payments of certain benefits. The general effect of the agreement is that residence in the one country is counted as residence or contributions in the other country when considering eligibility for a benefit.

(g) *Assistance for others in need:* Emergency benefits can be paid at the discretion of the Social Security Commission to persons suffering hardship who do not qualify statutorily for any of the above benefits; this allows complete flexibility of payment when needs could not otherwise be met.

War pensions

Disablement pensions, dependants' pensions, economic pensions, war veterans' allowances, war bursaries, medical treatment and funeral payments are available to ex-members of the New Zealand Armed Forces under a variety of conditions.

Supplementary assistance

Cash supplementation of benefits and pensions is available, subject to a full means-test, to persons who cannot meet necesary commitments out of current income or other resources. This assistance can be a continuing grant or a lump-sum grant. Additional welfare services are the supply of wheelchairs on loan, a home-help scheme, and a rest-home scheme for the aged in one district.

Social work

A team of social workers provides a casework and a counselling and guidance service for all persons in need of such help. The main areas of work are with broken homes, rehabilitation of the disabled, home management and family budgeting, unsettled migrants and refugees.

Cultural problems

(a) *The Maori:* As can be seen from the preceding summary, there are no apparent racial distinctions made in the administration of social security. However, fitting the Maori into the social security structure occasionally creates problems. At times there is difficulty in proving the age of the older Maori born before birth registration became compulsory in 1875. In making advances against Maori-owned land, difficulties can arise. In the past, Maori customary marriages have created difficulties, but departmental administration has now been modified to handle such cases easily. Investigations into the financial affairs of the Maori to test his eligibility for assistance are sometimes difficult and complicated. The Maori is at times most reluctant to discuss his affairs and can be suspicious of enquiries. Finally there is the urbanisation of the Maori of today bringing with it the tendency to overcommit with debts, mainly hire-purchase; tempting offers of low deposit and easy credit can lead to serious debt troubles if and when the family income suddenly drops to benefit level.

While today there is no discrimination on racial grounds in the social security administration, this state of affairs is comparatively recent. Until 1940, social security provided a lower rate of unemployment benefit to a Maori applicant who was living in the Pa. Until quite recently, the family benefit paid to a Maori mother in respect of her child was cancelled when the child left home; in the pakeha family this was not the case. Also until relatively recently, lump-sum grants of supplementary assistance in excess of £10 when granted to a Maori were invariably paid to an agent. Similar grants to pakehas were normally paid to the applicant unless the Department had sound reason to suspect that the money might be misused. At the present time however, all such differentiations have been removed.

(b) *The refugee:* Partly because of language difficulties and partly because of cultural differences, such as attitude to authority or family roles, the refugee may arrive in New Zealand with confused concepts of the Welfare State. He may be suspicious of close enquiries. He may not believe and accept his rights as a citizen. He may have been given overseas an incorrect interpretation of social security assistance available. He may have feelings of frustration at his ineligibility for permanent benefits until residence requirements have been met (this can make him seem differently treated from his New Zealand neighbour). However, these cases can be met where hardship is apparent by payment of emergency benefits or special refugee grants.

(c) *The British immigrant:* The immigrant who arrives in New Zealand with the background of a different social security system may tend to place his own interpretations on the New Zealand system. Reciprocity does not apply to all types of benefits and some of the conditions vary, but in general, serious problems are few.

(d) *Pacific Islanders:* The Cook Islanders come to New Zealand to seek employment. The general public tend to accept them as the Maori is accepted, but they have few qualifications for benefit assistance. Although Cook Islanders are New Zealand citizens they are not subject to New Zealand taxation until they arrive in New Zealand and they have no rights to social security until they have met the residential qualification. This, of course, can create serious problems in the event of sickness or unemployment shortly after arrival, but cases of hardship are helped under supplementary assistance or emergency benefits.

Fijians and Samoans are not New Zealand citizens and are treated on the same basis as any other persons arriving in New Zealand who have to wait until they qualify under the residential provision for benefits. However, again in cases of hardship they can be helped under emergency benefits or supplementary assistance.

(e) *Asians:* Chinese and Indians and other Asians who settle in New Zealand are also not eligible for assistance until they qualify under the normal residential qualifications.

Training

It can be said that in New Zealand training for social work includes a reasonable concentration on cross-cultural matters. To do his job efficiently the social worker must have a reasonable knowledge of the cultural background of the Maori. This knowledge also extends to other cultural groups who are settled in New Zealand. Education in racial problems is therefore an integral part of social work training.

General comment

From this brief summary it will be apparent that the present social security system is sufficiently flexible to meet the main objective of providing acceptable income security to the whole population regardless of race, colour, or creed. At no time is there official discrimination and the criteria for assistance endeavour to ignore any cultural differences which may exist.

APPENDIX 'B'

THE MAORI WELFARE DIVISION

The activities of the Department, directed as they are to the welfare of the Maori race, interlock the activities of the Welfare Division with those of every other division of the Department necessitating very close liaison and cooperation among all departmental officers.

The Welfare Division had its birth in the Maori Social and Economic Advancement Act 1945, although there had been some move towards a welfare group in the early thirties, when three men were appointed to work in districts where the people were backward in accepting the Department's policy of land development and settlement. Their task was to persuade the people to join the scheme and to offer their land for development.

Under the Maori Social and Economic Advancement Act, provision was made for the Tribal Executives and Committees, formed to assist in the war effort, to be reorganised and for Maori Welfare Officers to be appointed as members of the Department of Maori Affairs. Tribal Executives exercised control over areas contained in tribal districts, their membership consisting of two representatives of each Tribal Committee together with the Maori Welfare Officer for the area as an ex officio member. The Tribal Committees were elected by the Maori public to administer a settlement or group of settlements. This administration extended to everything pertaining to the welfare of the Maori race or to an individual member of the race.

In 1961, an amendment to the Act provided for the setting up of both District and National Maori Councils, as a means of two-way communication between the Government and the Maori people on matters of moment to both.

The Maori Social and Economic Advancement Act was repealed by the passing of the Maori Welfare Act 1962. This consolidated the earlier Act and under its provisions Maori Associations became independent of the Department.

The Maori Welfare Division and the Maori Associations are governed by the Maori Welfare Act 1962. It provides for the constitution of Maori Associations, defines their powers and functions, and defines the general functions of the Minister, the Secretary, Welfare Officers, Honorary Welfare Officers and Maori Wardens in relation to the social and economic advancement of the Maori people.

A brief summary of the Maori Welfare Act 1962 is as follows:

(a) The Minister of Maori Affairs administers the Act.

(b) The Secretary directs and controls the general functions of both Welfare Officers and Honorary Welfare Officers.

(c) Welfare Officers are appointed as members of the Department of Maori Affairs under the State Services Act 1962.

(d) Honorary Welfare Officers are appointed or removed from office by the Minister.

(e) Maori Committees, Executives and Councils are fully independent and their members are elected by the Maori people themselves.

The objective of the Welfare Division is to assist the Maori to take and maintain his rightful place in the community. In striving for this objective the policies of the Division are to help the Maori people in respect of their general welfare, particularly their education, housing, vocational training, employment and health.

The Division collaborates with and gives such assistance and advice to Maori Associations and other groups as may be necessary or helpful so that the people themselves may find and apply their own solutions to their own problems and develop and achieve the utmost satisfaction from their own culture. The Division also collaborates with appropriate social welfare agencies, State and voluntary, to help individuals and families who are having difficulty adapting themselves to a new social and economic environment.

The services of the Maori Welfare Division are for the handicapped rather than for those who are capable of helping themselves. A Maori capable of helping himself is encouraged and indeed made to conduct his own affairs and to use the normal services available.

Though it is difficult if not impossible to establish a hard and fast rule by which it can be judged that this job of work is relevant and that that is not, some general system of determination is necessary. This can be stated broadly as follows:

(a) where a State organisation is already established to perform certain stated functions, a Maori problem coming within that field is basically not the responsibility of the Maori Welfare Division; but

(b) where it is evident that a case would make progress only by the continued participation of the Maori Welfare Officer, then assistance is given.

Some of the main functions are summarised as follows:

Housing: The Welfare Officers' main function in housing is to stress on every opportune occasion the importance of better housing and by wise counselling encourage all Maoris, especially those in sub-standard conditions, to save and apply for housing assistance. Special attention is given to young and newly married couples and those intending to marry, to encourage them to build up a housing deposit by assignment of wages or to join a lay-by home ownership scheme. In some cases it may be decided that the alternative of a State rental house is preferable to home ownership.

Where assistance is granted, follow-up work is required by the Welfare Officer to ensure that the family realise the responsibilities of home ownership, the need for furnishing wisely, and proper budgeting. On this latter point it may be necessary for the Welfare Officer to introduce a client to the local Household Budgeting Advisory Service which has been actively fostered by the Department. The Household Budgeting Advisory Service referred to began in an organised way in 1960 at Kaikohe when a group of private citizens formed a Citizens' Advice and Guidance Council to provide budgeting and other advice to people in need of it. The movement has spread to a number of centres of varying size, mainly in the North Island.

The primary objective of the Service is to enable clients to fit their expenditure to their income and thus ultimately become independent, self-reliant members of the community.

Education: The Department's aim is to ensure that Maoris take full advantage of the opportunities offering for education and vocational advancement and to assist professional officers to build up their knowledge and understanding of the Maori people.

The work of Welfare Officers in this field is predominantly in the home, the community and with the parents. Educational guidance of pupils and advisory work are functions of the education authorities—teachers, careers advisers, guidance counsellors and the Education Department officers.

The Welfare Officer encourages pre-school training, school entry at five years of age, and regular attendance at school. In this work he often functions in liaison with Maori groups, education specialists, and the Maori Education Foundation, a body which has been set up to encourage the better education of Maoris and to provide financial assistance. The provision of reports for the Maori Education Foundation has now become an important part of Welfare Officers' duties.

In the schools (both primary and secondary), the Welfare Officer is expected to get to know personally the staff (particularly head teachers) in their zone with large Maori rolls. Head teachers are made aware that when faced with problems of special difficulty involving Maori pupils, the services of the Welfare Division are readily available on request. In reaching a solution to these problems, the Welfare Officer may call on the services of other organisations, community groups and individuals as appropriate.

Vocational guidance and placement: The objective here is to encourage and assist all Maori pupils to continue with formal education while they are able to derive benefit from it and to place to best advantage those who are ready to leave school. The role of the Welfare Officer in the community is by working through Maori Committees, Maori Women's Welfare League branches and other community groups to take active steps to educate parents and the Maori people generally not only on the expert services available to their children in the way of educational and vocational guidance and job placement, but also on the types of jobs available.

Employment: In employment, the aim is to ensure that every opportunity is taken to place Maoris in employment suitable to their capabilities and educational attainments. While the Department of Labour has the statutory responsibility in their field, Welfare Officers also assist by establishing liaison with large firms requiring labour and thus do much useful work in placement.

The Department's general role is much wider than placement. It is establishing and maintaining good relations with employers, employment agencies, employee organisations and the like, helping to curb the incidence of absenteeism on the part of those placed, maintaining contact with groups, particularly youth groups and those relocated, encouraging young people to study and obtain qualifications—in short, carrying out the range of activities incidental to employment that foster on the one hand the successful social adjustment of the worker and on the other a fuller understanding by employers and the community of the problems the Maori is facing at the present time.

To Maori boys who prefer manual labour, the advantages of apprenticeship are pointed out. In addition, to assist Maori youth, the Department has established trade-training schemes in Auckland, Wellington and Christchurch in carpentry, plumbing, electrical-wiring, motor mechanics, panelbeating, painting and decorating, and plastering.

Pre-employment courses: Special pre-employment courses for 35 boys and 25 girls were introduced by the Department in conjunction with the Wellington Polytechnic in January 1966. This new scheme is designed to help young Maoris from rural areas to adjust themselves to city life. The courses were of five weeks' duration and included tuition in basic English and mathematics as well as civic-social studies. Visits were arranged to different types of jobs and at the end of the courses the students were placed in permanent employment. Similar courses will be provided early each year.

Hostels: The progressive expansion of the Department's trade training schemes, and the need to provide suitable accommodation for the increasing number of other Maori school leavers who have to find jobs away from their home districts, have created a constant demand for more hostels in the main centres such as Auckland, Wellington and Christchurch. Over the last two years the Department has added new wings to a number of hostels and purchased one large property for this purpose. It has also built flats for single girls and young women in some of the main centres.

Relocation: In the movement of Maori people from rural to urban areas, the Welfare Division is fully involved in the job of relocation—in seeing to re-employment, accommodation and all the work in assisting the family to settle in the new area.

Health: Although the Health Department has the prime responsibility for Maori health and provides the leadership and professional knowledge, the Department of Maori Affairs needs to maintain close liaison with the Health Department to supply background material on local people and their attitudes and to advise on special techniques required when communicating with the Maori people.

In the field of physical welfare, the role of the Welfare Division is to stimulate and to encourage participation of all young Maoris in sporting, recreational and cultural activities, whether sponsored by Maori, European, local body or other groups in the community.

Welfare Officers also investigate reports on anti-social behaviour, and difficult homes; they assist police, and counsel erring families. In Court work, they ascertain whether legal aid is required and arrange this where necessary. They are also called on frequently to deal with adoption applications for Maoris under the provisions of the Adoptions Amendment Act 1962.

Honorary Welfare Officers: Honorary Welfare Officers are appointed by the Minister under Section 5 of the Welfare Act 1962. They are not public servants but voluntary workers. Each Honorary Welfare Officer on appointment receives specific directions as to the area he serves and the functions he performs. An Honorary Welfare Officer has the same powers and functions as a departmental Welfare Officer within the area in respect of which he is appointed.

Experience has shown that it is more satisfactory for all concerned if an Honorary Welfare Officer is given a fairly circumscribed task in a particular field. Duties are similar to the departmental officer's but the range is restricted to a small area and to a specialised function. Examples of work which are allocated to an Honorary Welfare Officer are:

In the education field: he may be allocated a particular school or a particular facet of work associated with schools in a defined area, for example, absenteeism, social problems, advisory work with professional staff.

Working with offenders: he may be asked to attend regularly at a Court to counsel on the advisability of legal aid and to assist other workers in this field.

Working with young people: he may be asked to promote youth clubs or to work closely with one already established.

On the other hand an officer may show a marked preference for certain types of welfare work in which he or she has had previous experience. Special skills of this kind are of course exploited.

APPENDIX 'C'

THE ADMINISTRATION OF JUSTICE

The responsibility of the Department of Justice is to treat all persons under its care, firstly according to the sentence of the Court, and secondly according to their specific needs. As a matter of deliberate policy, there is no separate treatment or institution for Maoris or non-Maoris. The staff of the probation service and penal institutions include Europeans, Maoris and Rarotongans without distinction as to duties and responsibilities. Maori prison officers conduct discussion groups composed of non-Maoris and Maoris. A Maori chaplain counsels all inmates in the Detention Centre regardless of race, and Maori counsellors work in Waikeria and Invercargill Borstals.

The appointment of Maori counsellors is in line with the Department's policy to extend its counselling service and is also a recognition of particular Maori problems. These problems are related to social factors rather than to racial personality characteristics. The same services and personnel are available to probationers and inmates of all races.

APPENDIX 'D'

THE ROLE AND RESOURCES OF THE CHILD WELFARE DIVISION

Role

The Division, then called the Branch, was established by the Child Welfare Act, 1925, the purpose of which was:

> To make better provision with respect to the maintenance, care and control of children who are under the protection of the State; and to provide generally for the protection and training of indigent, neglected and delinquent children.

To carry out this purpose, the Child Welfare Branch and the Children's Court were established. The work done by the Division to fulfil its functions can be briefly described as follows:

—Investigating and reporting on all cases involving children under 17 (or under 18 in some cases) coming before the Children's Court either as a result of an offence (except murder or manslaughter) or following a legal complaint that a child is neglected, indigent, not under proper control, delinquent or living in an environment detrimental to his physical or moral wellbeing.

—The subsequent care in short stay homes, in longer stay institutions and in foster-homes of children who, for reasons of neglect, poor environment or difficult behaviour, are placed by the Children's Court under the guardianship of the Superintendent of the Child Welfare Division.

—The subsequent oversight (usually in their own homes) of children placed by the Children's Court under our supervision but not under our guardianship; this involves regular interviews with the children and parents, cooperation with the school, helping to arrange suitable work where required, arranging club and other such contacts and visits to medical, psychological and psychiatric specialists, where necessary.

—Preventive work with children and families in an endeavour to avoid Court action. This necessitates, in the early stages of trouble, help of a similar nature to the above and includes financial aid if needed.

—Cooperation with officers of the Juvenile Crime Prevention Section of the N.Z. Police in an attempt to deal with delinquency where possible on a preventive basis and without court action. Child Welfare Officers undertake oversight of cases where preventive supervision is considered appropriate.

—Attending to a wide variety of miscellaneous duties involving inquiries into cases of truancy, complaints from many sources regarding children and reports to other agencies and Departments.

—Administration of homes and institutions for children, including residential schools for deaf and backward children.

—Placement and oversight of immigrant and refugee children. Inquiries into illegitimate births to ensure that proper provision is being made for the child and for the mother where necessary.

—Reporting to Courts on applications for adoption of children, and on matrimonial proceedings affecting custody of children.

—Licensing of foster-parents who for payment or reward keep children under six years of age in their homes for more than seven consecutive days. These foster-homes are visited and the care of the children supervised.

—Inspection of Children's Homes run by voluntary organisations, and administration of financial assistance by way of capitation subsidy for each child cared for and a subsidy of up to 50 percent on expenditure for extension or replacement of buildings or additions to facilities. Advisory help is also offered to the managements and staffs of these Homes.

—Licensing and supervision of child care centres (commonly referred to as 'day nurseries') in order to ensure that adequate standards are maintained.

Resources

The Child Welfare Division is a Division of the Department of Education. It is properly an educational and not a law enforcement agency. For some years now Ministerial responsibility has been divided (by Cabinet arrangement but not by statute) between the Minister of Education and the Minister in Charge of the Child Welfare Division. The Director-General of Education is responsible to the Minister of Education for the general administration of the Division. Although the Superintendent of Child Welfare is responsible to the Director-General on administrative matters, he exercises his own discretion on decisions within his power as guardian of State wards. The statute is precise on this; the Superintendent acts 'to the exclusion of all other persons'.

The Division consists of administrative, field, institution and clerical workers. National administration is the function of Head Office, situated in Wellington, and comprises the Superintendent who is responsible to the Director-General of Education for the work of the Child Welfare Division, a Deputy Superintendent, a Supervisor of Institution Services, a Supervisor of Field Services, a Senior Inspector, two Inspectors, a Supervisor of Registered Children's Homes and Child Care Centres, a Senior Boys' Welfare Officer, a Senior Child Welfare Officer, an Executive Officer, an Assistant Executive Officer and other clerical officers.

Field work is carried out in 29 districts from Kaitaia to Invercargill. Each district is under the local administrative control of a District Child Welfare Officer and in addition comprises men and women field officers, called Boys' Welfare Officers and Child Welfare Officers respectively, as well as clerical officers, the numbers in each category depending on the size of the district. There are approximately 270 men and women field officers and 235 clerical officers. In addition 150 Honorary Child Welfare Officers give valuable assistance to the salaried officers, the type and extent of help given by individuals varying with their personal circumstances.

The Division employs approximately 400 institution officers in a variety of institutions designed to meet the special needs of children under care.

There are 12 short-term institutions comprising six Receiving Homes for girls and small boys at Auckland, Hamilton, Palmerston North, Wellington, Christchurch and Dunedin, five Boys' Homes for boys aged approximately seven to 17 at Auckland, Hamilton, Lower Hutt, Christchurch and Dunedin, and a Girls' Home in Auckland to cater for more difficult adolescent girls. These institutions, which are under the control of the District Child Welfare Officer in the particular centre, are for short-term training usually leading to early foster home or employment placement or, where necessary, placement in an institution providing prolonged special training.

There are eight longer term institutions catering for special needs:

—Schools for the Deaf in Kelston, Auckland and Sumner, Christchurch.
—Campbell Park School, Otekaike (near Oamaru), and Salisbury Girls' School, Richmond (near Nelson), for intellectually retarded children aged approximately 10 to 17 years of age.
—A Training Centre for boys, Kohitere, at Levin, and a Training Centre for girls, Kingslea, in Christchurch, for difficult and delinquent children who require long-term training.

—Fareham House, Featherston, provides educational and social training for girls aged approximately 12 to 14 years.

—The Mt. Wellington Residential School, Auckland, for children aged approximately seven to 14 years who are so disturbed emotionally that they are unable to profit from attending an ordinary school.

The manager, Kohitere, and principals, Kingslea and Fareham House, are responsible to the Superintendent of Child Welfare for all matters connected with the operation of their institutions. Principals of special schools for deaf and backward children are responsible to the Superintendent except in educational matters for which they are responsible to the Director-General of Education. The pattern of administration for the Mt. Wellington Residential School is similar to that which applies to the other special schools.

A Girls' Hostel at Wadestown, Wellington, caters for a small group of working State wards who require closer supervision than can readily be provided in a board placement in the community.

Throughout the country there are a number of Family Homes operated by husband and wife and each capable of accommodating approximately five or six children. These Homes are under the control of the local District Child Welfare Officer.

Judicial Limitations

Only the Court can deprive parents of guardianship. Child Welfare Officers are not entitled to act arbitrarily. This has a bearing on two common criticism of Child Welfare work, namely:

(i) that Child Welfare Officers have not taken drastic action to remove a child from home, when someone has suggested that this be done, and

(ii) that Child Welfare Officers take children away from their parents without adequate justification.

The answer to both criticisms is that, before a child can be taken away from his parents' guardianship, a convincing case, based on admissible evidence, must be submitted to the Court justifying it making an Order. In emergencies, a child can be removed hurriedly from home on the authority of a warrant, but the warrant must be followed by Court action.

Index